"In our day the Christian faith is (not for the first time but for the first time in many centuries) truly ecumenical; that is, it reflects the whole inhabited world in its cultural and linguistic diversity. One of the many merits of this fine book is that it demonstrates that the crucial issues for contemporary Christians arise directly from this fact; and that, for Western Christians in particular, they involve renewal of vision and shifting of focus, a conversion of habits of mind and association. There are now many surveys of world Christianity, but few of them grapple, as this one does, with the immediate and practical implications of the transformation of the Christian church."

— ANDREW F. WALLS
Liverpool Hope University
Akrofi-Christaller Institute of
Theology, Mission and Culture

"A timely and discerning interpretation of current developments in world Christianity. . . . Knowing that a process is under way and coming to terms with it are two different things. Granberg-Michaelson presents not just what God may be doing with the Christianity of the global South and East but also how he expects interest groups like the WCC to respond. This will definitely be mandatory reading for my students of non-Western Christianity."

— J. KWABENA ASAMOAH-GYADU
Trinity Theological Seminary,
Accra, Ghana

"Over the past decade, we have seen many books that announce the rise of Christianity from the global South and East, but this new book by Wes Granberg-Michaelson is different. Yes, world Christianity is here, he says — but now what? . . . Offering wise and winsome advice for inter-cultural fellowship and partnership, this book is both eye-opening and deeply practical. I hope it provokes fresh Christian thinking and engagement, far and wide."

— JOEL CARPENTER
Nagel Institute for the Study
of World Christianity,
Calvin College

"Granberg-Michaelson describes with great skill how the demographic shift of Christianity to the global South over the past hundred years has transformed the faith. In the process, he asks penetrating questions about its seemingly intractable divisions and unrelenting fragmentation. His proposal for unity in the midst of this chaos comes from a deeply personal and compelling vision for Christians to share their common pilgrimage. Only then, he notes, will the global church be truly effective in offering hope and reconciliation to our divided world."

— TODD M. JOHNSON
Gordon-Conwell
Theological Seminary

From Times Square to Timbuktu

*The Post-Christian West Meets the
Non-Western Church*

Wesley Granberg-Michaelson

WILLIAM B. EERDMANS PUBLISHING COMPANY
GRAND RAPIDS, MICHIGAN / CAMBRIDGE, U.K.

Published 2013 by
Wm. B. Eerdmans Publishing Co.
2140 Oak Industrial Drive N.E., Grand Rapids, Michigan 49505 /
P.O. Box 163, Cambridge CB3 9PU U.K.

Printed in the United States of America

18 17 16 15 14 13   7 6 5 4 3 2 1

Library of Congress Cataloging-in-Publication Data

Granberg-Michaelson, Wesley.
From Times Square to Timbuktu: the post-Christian West meets
the non-western church / Wesley Granberg-Michaelson.
        pages   cm
Includes bibliographical references and index.
ISBN 978-0-8028-6968-5 (pbk.: alk. paper)
1. Christianity — 21st century.   I. Title.

BR121.3.G73   2013
270.8′3 — dc23
2013011137

www.eerdmans.com

To Hubert van Beek
A faithful colleague and
persistent ecumenical pioneer

Contents

Foreword, by James H. Billington   ix

Acknowledgments   xi

Prologue   xiii

1. The Pilgrimage of Christianity   1

2. How the World Is Changing Christianity   7

3. What Divides World Christianity   13

4. God's Heart for Unity   28

5. Roads Well Traveled   44

6. New Pathways   58

7. Signposts along the Way   70

8. Christians on the Move   79

9. Word Becoming Flesh, Congregationally   96

10. Under the Ecclesiological Radar   117

11. "In Each Place . . . and in All Places"   126

12. The Spirit and the World in the Twenty-first Century   137

Epilogue: The View from Ghana   153

Bibliography   162

Index   166

Foreword

The modern Western study of demography and development in the non-Western world generally neglects the subject of religion. Our mainstream opinion makers often seem to suggest that religion itself is both sustaining backwardness and promoting violent extremism in what we used to call the Third World.

This succinct and readable book by Wesley Granberg-Michaelson tells us a very different story. It is a reality check about how, within the world's largest religion, the post-Christian West is meeting the non-Western church. Granberg-Michaelson provides both

1. a brief history of how the worshiping center of global Christianity has moved from the Northern Hemisphere to the Southern Hemisphere; and
2. a plea for American churches to develop new, multicultural communities of faith with the many diverse Christians now migrating from the South to the North.

Granberg-Michaelson writes from a rich background of Christian experience as the former head of the Reformed Church in America, as a key staff leader for the World Council of Churches in Geneva, and as a charter participant in a new international and non-hierarchical ecumenical movement. But he is writing here as a descriptive analyst reflecting on existing statistics — not as a proselytizing theologian or philosophical critic of contemporary culture.

Granberg-Michaelson sees post-Western Christianity as creating a variety of emotionally expressive local communities rather than new denominations. The new southern center of Christianity is also "re-drawing the boundaries" that in the West have separated out the material from the spiritual world. He tends to relate all this to the broader phenomenon in the Southern Hemisphere of moving beyond all its past dependencies — not just away from distant colonial overlords, but also beyond more recent home-grown dictators who cloak themselves with demagogic, secular nationalism.

Granberg-Michaelson advocates for America a genuine pluralism, not defined by elites who take for granted a secularized view of the world, but created to include the wide range of religious voices and worldviews that are now making America their home. This is arguably not too far from the basic view of almost all of our founders that pluralism meant a plurality of authentic convictions in and about religion, not a monism of indifference verging on hostility to religion itself.

JAMES H. BILLINGTON
Librarian of Congress

Acknowledgments

While anecdotes and personal observations prompted my curiosity about the themes of this book, I became eager to learn more about the trends and facts reshaping the presence of Christianity around the world. The John W. Kluge Center at the Library of Congress provided an extraordinary opportunity for me to do so in the fall of 2012. Housed within the historic Jefferson Building of the Library, the Center brings scholars from around the world to utilize the resources of the Library and interact with policy-makers and others in the capital. My deepest gratitude goes to Dr. James Billington, Librarian of the Congress, who appointed me as a Distinguished Visiting Scholar at the John W. Kluge Center in order to do the research and writing that resulted in this book.

Carolyn Brown, Director of the John W. Kluge Center, and its staff, including Jason Steinhauer, Travis Hensley, and Mary Lou Reker, provided consistent and valuable support. Cheryl Adams, a research librarian specializing in the religious collections of the Library of Congress, was a helpful guide in my work. The incredible resources of the Library provided a depth of exploration, particularly around the global patterns of migration and their effects on religious life, which could not have been duplicated elsewhere.

While I was in Washington, D.C., to do this work, Jim and Joy Wallis and their sons Luke and Jack offered me their gracious hospitality. Each day of reading and writing at the Library ended with a place to be at home with a warm and loving family. And often, what I discovered during the day was processed in discussions with Jim long into the evening, except during the World Series and on election night. I'm deeply grateful to the whole Wallis family.

In June of 2012, I had the honor of delivering lectures at the Horace G. Underwood Symposium in Seoul, Korea. Underwood, a graduate of New Brunswick Theological Seminary, was among the first Protestant missionaries to Korea. Dr. Gregg Mast, the seminary's current president, and Dr. Sou-Young Lee, Senior Pastor of the Saemoonan Church in Seoul, were my hosts. Those lectures and dialogue focused on the present global challenges to Christian unity and provided a solid foundation for addressing those issues in this book.

Lamin Sanneh, Andrew Walls, Jehu Hanciles, and Philip Jenkins have all done pioneering work in describing the history and trends shaping world Christianity and its implications for the future. I have been deeply inspired by the pathways of understanding they have opened for others to follow.

Once again, I've had the thoroughly enjoyable experience of working on this book with Jon Pott, Editor in Chief at Eerdmans Publishing. His editorial judgment has been consistently accurate, and his friendship has been a source of ongoing encouragement throughout this project.

Finally, the strongest advocate for my writing this book has been my wife Karin. She had the wisdom to know how valuable my time at the Library of Congress would be even before I did, and the generosity to support my work there even while she remained doing her ministry in Grand Rapids. That made all the difference, and I'm so deeply grateful to her.

Prologue

The New York taxi was taking me from Midtown Manhattan, near Times Square, to the Interchurch Center at 475 Riverside Drive, often called the "God Box." This structure was built to house most U.S. mainline denominational offices and ecumenical agencies, although several have since moved out of the city. I was speaking that day to one of the remaining denominational agencies on the changes in world Christianity, and the new challenges posed to Christian unity.

My friendly taxi driver, I learned, was from Ghana. So I asked him if he happened to attend a church. Enthusiastically he told me he did. So was it, perhaps, a congregation from the Presbyterian Church of Ghana, or something similar? No. Well then, I asked, was it a congregation more Pentecostal or charismatic in style? Yes, most definitely!

His congregation, he explained, was made up almost exclusively of Ghanaians and had a lively, vibrant worship, Bible study, healing ministry, and outreach. While it was independent, there were deep ties to particular congregations back in Ghana. Once in a while, the driver shared, he also attended a large, multicultural congregation in Times Square comprised of those from many nations around the world.

Delighted to meet a pastor who had visited his country, the driver dropped me at my destination. He had never heard of the Interchurch Center and the church agencies it housed. In the few steps I took from that taxi to the door of that building, I traversed a growing gulf in world Christianity.

I felt compelled to write this book to describe the dimensions of this gulf, to explore its implications for the life of the church both globally and locally, and to discover bridges that could cross vast cultural, theological, geographical distances. Sometimes that feels like going "from here to Timbuktu."

A city in Mali˙rich in Islamic scholarly history, Timbuktu became a metaphor in the West for a faraway place shrouded in mystery. So it's ironic that this city is now at the statistical center of gravity for world Christianity. This amplifies Timbuktu's metaphorical meaning as a powerful geographical illustration of world Christianity's rapid shift to the global South. Times Square might feel like the center of the universe to many, but if you're searching for the spot on the globe that's in the geographical center of the world's growing number of Christians, you'll end up on the western fringe of the Sahara in Africa.

The most dramatic illustration of this change, however, came when the words *"Habemus Papam"* were announced and Archbishop Jorge Bergoglio from Argentina emerged as Pope Francis, the first non-European pope in more than 1,200 years. Yet, most congregations in North America have little awareness of how these global changes are arriving at their own doorstep through patterns of immigration.

Back in a taxi, this time in Washington, D.C., my driver told me he's one of about 250,000 Ethiopians living in the Washington, D.C., area. They worship at thirty-five different Ethiopian churches. He attends one of the five Ethiopian Coptic Orthodox Churches in the nation's capital. But these facts on the ground are so out of sight to the political, cultural, and even religious elites in Washington that they might as well be in Timbuktu.

So the contours of world Christianity are changing in ways that plead for the radical attentiveness of congregations in North America. As global shifts create new local realities, the church can discover fresh pathways for fashioning a vital missional presence within the culture. But this requires that our eyes are opened to new visions of the unity of the body of Christ, and that we are empowered by the Spirit to confront all those forces that so shamefully divide us.

When the Spirit at Pentecost creatively formed believers into a community of faith, it empowered them to see all reality through a new lens. A similar epiphany is needed today to apprehend the new thing that is happening in the journey of world Christianity. Beyond the facts and reflections found on these pages, my hope is that we may be empowered spiritually to embrace new realities appearing unexpectedly in our midst, even in taxicabs near Times Square.

CHAPTER ONE

The Pilgrimage of Christianity

The Thomas Jefferson Building of the Library of Congress rests across the street from the U.S. Capitol, and next to the Supreme Court. Opened in 1897, it's a stunning example of Italian Renaissance design. Its Great Hall, at the front entrance, has a stained glass, decorated ceiling seventy-five feet above the marble floor, with names of leading thinkers in the history of the world on vaults that stretch toward the top. It almost has the feel of a cathedral honoring the intellectual progress of the modern Western world.

At the end of the Great Hall opposite the entrance, past the Commemorative Arch, two of the most valuable treasures of the Library of Congress are on display. On the right is the Giant Bible of Mainz. It is a magnificent example of the text of the Bible copied onto pages and bound together in a process that took fifteen months to complete. On the left is a Gutenberg Bible. This, of course, was the first book in Europe printed with movable type. Both of these Bibles were produced in Mainz, Germany, in the mid-1450s. But the technological difference between them is a hinge point of history, dramatically altering the pilgrimage of Christianity.

Bibles produced like the Giant Bible of Mainz — laboriously copied by hand — kept the text of Scripture in the hands of well-educated clergy, as well as princes and nobles with enough money to pay for one. Before the advent of the printing press, the literacy rate among males in Europe was from about 5 percent to 10 percent. But following Gutenberg's innovation, literacy rates rose to about 50 percent. The words of the Bible became far more accessible. As Gutenberg himself said, "Religious truth is captive in a small number of little manuscripts, which

1

guard the common treasures instead of expanding them. Let us break the seal which binds these holy things; let us give wings to truth that it may fly with the Word, no longer prepared at vast expense, but multiplied everlastingly by a machine which never wearies — to every soul which enters life!"[1]

The century that followed marked a decisive turn in the pilgrimage of Christianity. The democratization of the Bible dramatically altered patterns of authority, power, and governance in the life of the church. The Christian story was no longer communicated primarily through images, seen in the stained glass windows and paintings designed to capture the spiritual imagination of those worshiping in cathedrals. Now, growing numbers of people were reading directly from the text as literacy rates improved.

By the beginning of the sixteenth century, printing presses had expanded so rapidly throughout Europe that an estimated 20 million volumes of printed books and materials had been produced. All this was foundational to the spread of the Protestant Reformation that followed Martin Luther's posting of his Ninety-five Theses on the door of the Castle Church in Wittenberg, Germany, in 1517. The Reformation spread through the widespread printing of pamphlets and books as well as the increased access to the Bible itself.

Today, with the full Bible translated into at least 450 languages, and parts of Scripture translated into more than 2,500 tongues, hundreds of millions of the world's Christians read and study their own Bibles. With continuing technological change, those words are now held in smart phones and iPads. We take for granted this personalized, electronically ubiquitous access to Scripture. Yet, for the first 1,500 years of Christianity, the direct and personal availability of the Bible to any faithful believer was virtually unknown. This change marked a whole new trajectory in the pilgrimage of Christianity.

We tend to assume that Christianity is static rather than dynamic. Certainly most would agree that a core of Christian convictions, such as those formulated by the Apostles' Creed and other ancient creeds of the church, has remained as a consistent and unchanging articulation of Christian faith through the ages. Yet the forms and expressions of the faith, modes of worship, systems of government, interpretations of the

---

1. Bard Thompson, *The Modern Age* (Pensacola, Fla.: Beka Book Publications, 1981), p. 30.

Bible, understandings of theology, and contents of witness are end-lessly dynamic. The astonishing ability of Christian faith to embed its truth in the life of widely diverse and endlessly changing cultures is the key to its growth, durability, and vitality through time and across geographical space. Christianity rests on the conviction that God became flesh and blood in Jesus. This incarnational foundation projects Christianity into an ongoing pilgrimage, constantly asking how it finds expression and vital witness in the world's changing history and cultures.

Lamin Sanneh is a professor of missions and world Christianity at Yale Divinity School, and the author of numerous books and articles on the changes in global Christianity as well as the history of relationships between Christians and Muslims, particularly in Africa. His insights into the historical interplay of faith and culture, and his ability to describe the changing face of Christianity throughout the globe, are rich and utterly remarkable.[2]

In January of 2011 we were together in Istanbul at a meeting preparing for the forthcoming world gathering of the Global Christian Forum. Dr. Sanneh described the qualities that have allowed Christianity to endlessly grow, adapt, and express itself within an ever-changing array of cultural and historical contexts. In an insightful way, he contrasted this with Islam, pointing out how its faith is rooted in specific geographical places — Mecca and Medina, to which faithful Muslims are expected to make a holy pilgrimage in the course of their lifetimes. Further, Islam is deeply connected to a single language, Arabic. The Koran is memorized and recited around the world in Arabic, and translations of the Koran into other languages are not considered genuine and inspired expressions of its truths.

By contrast, Christian faith became detached from its geographical center in Jerusalem within its first two generations. Already in the New Testament, the church spread to the cosmopolitan city of Antioch, which became the center of its missionary outreach throughout the Roman Empire. While two thousand years of history include Jerusalem "falling" and being destroyed by enemies, and then being recaptured in ongoing conflicts through the centuries, the vitality and growth of Christian faith were not dependent on the status of its geographical origins. Similarly, Christian faith quickly became detached from a particu-

---

2. See especially Lamin Sanneh, *Disciples of All Nations: Pillars of World Christianity* (Oxford: Oxford University Press, 2008).

lar language. And of course, the decisive event in shaping the understanding and formative missional impulse of Christianity was its movement from Jewish culture to Greek culture, a drama that was at the core of the emerging church's development, and was recounted in the New Testament.

Lamin Sanneh's explanation underscores how Christianity has been on a continuous pilgrimage, moving with remarkable adaptability between languages and cultures, and never being bound to a specific place, region, or race. Of course, nations and civilizations have attempted to capture Christianity as their own, often with long-lasting, yet fallible, results. Our discussion took place in Istanbul, formerly Constantinople, the political and spiritual center of the Byzantine Empire until its fall to armies of the Ottoman Empire led by Sultan Mehmed II in 1453 — just two years before the Gutenberg Bible displayed in the Library of Congress was printed. So while the fall of Constantinople was a devastating geopolitical blow to Christendom, Christianity continued to move, adapt, reform, and even flourish during the next century in ways that could never have been imagined.

Christianity is in the midst of another dramatic pilgrimage today. Its most obvious expression is geographical. The center of world Christianity, in terms of the sheer numbers of Christians and the growth of their churches, has moved decisively to the Southern Hemisphere, or the global South. Over the past century, this astonishing shift in the globe's Christian population is the most dramatic geographical change that has happened in two thousand years of history.[3]

The truth of this demographic reality is just beginning to be grasped, especially by the Christian community in the United States and Europe. The consequences of this change are barely being imagined. Yet this probably constitutes another of those decisive hinge points in Christian history, with effects as potentially far-reaching as other times when the pilgrimage of Christianity has moved in radically new directions.

This shift is not simply about geography, with new maps revealing the changing global presence of the Christian community. It's also a

3. Todd M. Johnson, address given to the General Synod of the Reformed Church in America, June 24, 2012. This shift is thoroughly documented in Todd M. Johnson and Kenneth R. Ross, eds., *Atlas of Global Christianity, 1910-2010* (Edinburgh: Edinburgh University Press, 2009).

shift in the culture and mind-set shaping the expressions of Christian faith — changes far more difficult to map, but in the end, more decisive. So Christianity is not only moving from settled lands to new frontiers. It's also evolving from established forms and structures to fresh manifestations of its life, and from dogmatic systems to Spirit-filled discoveries.

The world today is witnessing a post-Western awakening of Christianity. The majority of Christians today are living in societies that have freed themselves from the colonial power of the West. They are fashioning expressions of faith that can appropriately be called "post-Western." So in many ways, we are witnessing the pilgrimage of Christianity as it moves out of the dominance of modern Western culture and beyond the framework of the modern Enlightenment.

The consequences of this transition will be far-reaching. Of course, several historic expressions of Christianity have never functioned in the framework of Western culture. But overall, we are witnessing a gravitational shift in Christianity's global presence moving away from northern, Western culture that has for long been its comfortable and formative cradle.

Of the many questions that focus our attention in following the present pilgrimage of Christianity, two shape the focus of this modest book. First, how will the historic attempts to build the unity of the church be affected by this shift? The modern ecumenical movement has been a major new and promising development in the life of the global church over the past century. But its task and challenges must become far more urgent, and require imaginative new approaches, for it to be carried forth in this rapidly and radically changing global Christian community.

Second, some effects of this non-Western awakening are already being felt in the West through global patterns of migration. As millions move from the Southern Hemisphere to the Northern Hemisphere, and from less affluent to more affluent societies, their Christian faith, with its cultural modes of expression and affiliation, comes with them. Thus, the religious landscape in North America and Europe is undergoing quiet but consequential change. Congregations there will be challenged in deep ways to explore what it means to live in fellowship and witness with Christian brothers and sisters whose faith has been shaped and formed by a far different cultural, economic, and spiritual fabric of experience.

Thus, Christianity is moving on its contemporary pilgrimage, seeking again those places that might become home. The varied expressions of the Christian family move in their particular ways, speeds, and directions. But it is critical at this historic point of transition that we learn how to journey together, creating and strengthening those fragile bonds of fellowship along the way. Despite the incredibly diverse and often bewildering expressions of Christian faith today, we are drawn into a common pilgrimage, where the challenge of accompanying one another becomes more difficult, but also more critically important, than ever.

Pilgrimages are as much about the journey as the destination. The point is not simply to get somewhere, but to expect that the process itself will reveal unexpected discoveries, test and nurture spiritual strength, build new relationships along the way, and strengthen our exercise of faith. So it is with the pilgrimage of Christianity in the world today. It requires attentiveness to whom we meet, openness to new understandings, and an unwavering trust that the Holy Spirit continues to prepare the way, guiding us into all truth. We are all called to follow on these paths, together.

CHAPTER TWO

How the World Is Changing Christianity

Christianity took centuries to move decisively to the global North. It's possible to locate throughout history the statistical center of world Christianity, that is, the point on the globe from which an equal number of Christians are found to the north, south, east, and west. Such information is among the vast resources found in the *Atlas of Global Christianity, 1910-2010,* edited by Todd M. Johnson and Kenneth R. Ross.[1]

For almost the whole first millennium of Christianity, its center of gravity was in west Asia, and a majority of Christians were in the global South. Around the year 600 Christianity began its clear pilgrimage toward the north and west, but it wasn't until sometime in the tenth century, almost a thousand years after Jesus was on the earth, that a majority of Christians found themselves living in those regions. By 1000, Christianity's statistical center had moved to a point near one of its great spiritual centers, Constantinople.

Five centuries later, in 1500, 92 percent of Christians were northern Europeans. But then world Christianity began a slow but steady path back toward the south. After four centuries, by 1900, its center of gravity had moved from Budapest, Hungary, its northernmost point, to Madrid, Spain, but still remained in the North. It was in the twentieth century that Christianity's geographic pilgrimage took the most pronounced, dramatic, and decisive change in direction in all its history. It rapidly accelerated its turn toward the south, and then also toward the east, and by 1980 there were more Christians in the global South than in

---

1. Todd M. Johnson and Kenneth R. Ross, eds., *Atlas of Global Christianity, 1910-2010* (Edinburgh: Edinburgh University Press, 2009).

7

the North for the first time in 1,000 years, and its center of gravity was in Africa.[2]

In 352 pages, the *Atlas of Global Christianity*, with countless maps and charts, supported by nearly fifty essays, presents the most comprehensive picture of the changes in Christianity in the last century. It takes as its starting point 1910, the time of the Edinburgh World Missionary Conference, and examines what happened in the pilgrimage of world Christianity in the following 100 years, ending in 2010.[3]

Some key facts summarize these changes:

In 1910, 66 percent of all Christians in the world lived in Europe; in 2010, only 26 percent lived there.

In 1910, only 2 percent of all Christians lived in Africa. Today, nearly one out of four Christians in the world is an African.

Europe and North America — the global North — contained 80 percent of all Christians in 1910, and only 40 percent a century later.

Christianity's statistical center by 2010 had moved to a point near Timbuktu, in Mali.

At the beginning of the last century, only a few million Christians were in Africa, less than 10 percent of Africa's population. That has grown to about 494 million adherents to Christianity, or almost 50 percent of the continent's population, and over 70 percent in sub-Saharan Africa. The Christian population of middle Africa was 1.1 percent in 1910, and has grown to 81.7 percent just a hundred years later. By the year 2025, the overall Christian population of Africa is projected to swell to 633 million.

The trajectory of Christianity's pilgrimage, seen through its statistical center of gravity, moved not only dramatically to the south in the last century, but beginning in 1970 it also began returning east. This was caused by the rising numbers of Christians in Asia. Christianity grew at twice the rate of overall population growth in Asia over the past century. China alone is estimated to have as many as 115 million Christians today. On any given Sunday, it is thought that more Christians are attending worship in congregations in China than in the United States.

---

2. Johnson and Ross, *Atlas of Global Christianity*, pp. 50-51.

3. The statistics that follow are taken from various charts and essays in the *Atlas of Global Christianity*.

Surprises continue. More recently, countries like Nepal and Cambodia have witnessed rapid growth. In the last decade, Christians in Nepal have grown by 4.6 percent. And after being nearly exterminated by Pol Pot, Christianity in Cambodia has grown by 7.2 percent in the last decade. Mongolia, once virtually closed to Christianity, now has blossoming and growing churches.

The Philippines was the only country in Asia with a majority Christian population — 86 percent — in 1910, due to three centuries of Spanish colonial rule ending in 1898. By 2010, its 83 million Christians constituted 89 percent of the population, with growth particularly among Protestant and independent churches. Indonesia, which holds the world's largest Muslim population, had growth in the number of Christians at twice the rate of overall population growth, although the Christian community remains a small minority.

In South Korea, Christianity has grown faster over the past century — at 6.17 percent — than anywhere else in Asia. From only about 50,000 Christians in 1910, the Korean church has grown to more than 20 million, about 41 percent of South Korea's population.[4] But that growth has subsided, with Korean churches barely maintaining their present percentage of overall population. In the last decade, the fastest growth of the church in Asia has come from China and Mongolia, as well as Cambodia and Nepal.

While 50 percent of the population in Asia was Buddhist in 1910, by 2010 that had dropped to 22 percent. The Muslim community has grown the fastest in that continent over the last century, with about 1 billion adherents comprising one-quarter of all Asians. Yet in the last decade, Christianity has grown at a rate of about 2.4 percent, faster than the growth of Muslims, at 1.7 percent. Christians in the Asian continent make up about 8.5 percent of the total population, but that figure represents 350 million people, and is projected to grow to 460 million by 2025.

In 1910, 95 percent of the population in Latin America was Christian, primarily through the presence of the Catholic Church that had accompanied Spanish and Portuguese colonial rule. Only 1 percent of the Christian population was non-Catholic. As the population of the conti-

---

4. Johnson and Ross, *Atlas of Global Christianity*, p. 140. Some Korean Christians dispute this figure, and place the percentage of Christians in their country as lower, at about 30 percent.

nent grew, so did the Christian community. But early in that century the traditional Protestant community began to grow.

The last fifty years, however, have seen the rapid and often astonishing growth of Pentecostalism in Latin America. During that time, it is estimated that 80 percent to 90 percent of Protestant growth has come from Pentecostals.[5] By 2010, Latin America was home to nearly 550 million Christians, and 20 percent were from non-Catholic expressions of Christian faith. These are growing at three times the rate of Catholic growth.[6] It has been reported, for instance, that forty new Pentecostal congregations are started each week in Rio de Janeiro.[7] By 2025, the Christian population in Latin America will grow to 640 million, or roughly the same as that of Africa.

This overall movement in world Christianity is also reflected in specific traditions. In 1910, for instance, North America and Europe were home to 90 percent of the world's evangelicals. But by 2010, that figure had been reduced to 25 percent, with 75 percent of evangelicals in the global South. The question facing all of Christianity is whether that shift is reflected in global patterns of power and decision making in its international organizations, and if it is, how it is reflected.

The same dynamics affect the Catholic Church, comprising almost one out of every two Christians in the world. Today, the countries with the largest numbers of Catholics are no longer Italy and France, as in 1910, but Brazil and Mexico. Further, the annual growth rate of Catholics in Africa in the twentieth century was 4.46 percent, which is faster than any other region. But the questions of power remain, demonstrated by Pope Benedict's appointment of 22 new cardinals, celebrated at the Vatican on February 18, 2012.

Of those 22, 18 were under the age of eighty, and thus eligible to vote for the next pope. Of those 18, 7 are Italians and 5 others are from Europe. Ten are Vatican officials. One new cardinal was chosen from India, Brazil, and Hong Kong. None were from Africa, where the Catholic Church is growing the fastest. Probably in response to criticism, in late October 2012 Pope Benedict announced the appointment of 6 additional cardinals — 1 each from the United States, Colombia, Nigeria,

---

5. Philip Jenkins, *The Next Christendom: The Coming of Global Christianity* (Oxford: Oxford University Press, 2002), p. 63.

6. Johnson and Ross, *Atlas of Global Christianity,* p. 188.

7. Jenkins, *The Next Christendom,* p. 64.

Lebanon, India, and the Philippines. But the balance of power in the college of cardinals among the 115 who entered the conclave in March 2013 to elect a new pope remained decisively in the global North — 60 were from Europe (of which 29 were from Italy), 14 from North America, 19 from South America (which holds about half of the world's Catholics), 11 from Africa, 10 from Asia, and 1 from Australia.[8] This made the election of Pope Francis from Argentina all the more remarkable.

The current pathways of Christianity's pilgrimage, while they can never be charted with certainty, nevertheless remain relatively clear. As Christianity continues to grow in Africa, Asia, and Latin America, by the end of this century, in 2100, Christians living in the global South and East will number 2.8 billion and be about three times more than the 775 million Christians projected to be found in the global North.[9]

In many ways, we're witnessing a return of Christianity to the non-Western cultures of Asia and Africa, reflecting more the environments that first gave rise to the church. But now, beginning from that initial transition from Jerusalem to Antioch, Christianity is embedded in hundreds of cultures and languages, demonstrating an incredible diversity of peoples and places that have received the incarnational presence of the gospel.

Many have told this story with persuasive and illuminating clarity. When Philip Jenkins published *The Next Christendom* in 2002, it quickly became a widely read work that brought many of these trends into focus, and reflected on their consequences. Missiologists and scholars like Andrew Walls have pioneered in interpreting the significance of these trends for understanding the global church. Lamin Sanneh, already mentioned, has probed the depths of Christianity's expression in non-Western culture in works like *Disciples of All Nations*.[10]

As my friend Joel Carpenter, director of the Nagel Institute for the Study of World Christianity at Calvin College, said to me, "The move of the center of Christianity to the global South is the new orthodoxy." Growing numbers of writers and researchers are focusing on these realities. Chairs and institutes for the study of world Christianity are begin-

---

8. Jean-Louis de la Vaissiere, "Pope's Surprise Announcement of Six New Cardinals," AFP, October 24, 2012: http://www.google.com/hostednews/afp/article/ALeqM5j8mAqsw RrGLbINe7Sk7gqRDrUdQA?docId=CN G.bc7a27cc16c26dd 349b374e3ed23be18.861.

9. Johnson and Ross, *Atlas of Global Christianity*, p. 188.

10. Lamin Sanneh, *Disciples of All Nations: Pillars of World Christianity* (Oxford: Oxford University Press, 2008).

ning to appear at seminaries and other institutions. Todd Johnson, coeditor of the *Atlas of Global Christianity*, summarizes the book's contents in a Power Point presentation with sixty-seven slides conveying its rich resources and presents it to interested groups and audiences throughout the country and world.

But we are just beginning to reflect on what the most dramatic shift in the history of Christianity's pilgrimage throughout the world means for our understanding of faith, and for the future of the church. Christians in the South and the East, leading the future of the world church, will begin to analyze and critique the dominance of Christianity by the culture and history of the West for the past thousand years. A new agenda of theological, ecclesiological, social, and economic questions will arise, and that process is already well under way.

Furthermore, the difficult reality to name is that the growth of Christianity in the global South is accompanied by its diminishment in the global North. As Andrew Walls has written, "Between the twentieth century and the present day, western Europe has moved from Christian heartland to Christian wasteland, and there has been a degree of withering in the West as a whole."[11] The dramatic regional growth of Christianity has been offset by a recession in the number of Christians relative to overall population in areas that held the majority of the world's Christians for the past thousand years. Thus the overall percentage of Christians in the world's population, which was 34.8 percent in 1910, has actually slightly decreased, to 33.2 percent in 2010.

The potential for sharp conflicts is severe between churches in the North, rooted for hundreds of years in faithful tradition, who strive to continue their witness amidst the forces of secularization, and young churches in the global South that are emboldened with spiritual enthusiasm and energy. The future course of Christianity's ongoing pilgrimage, then, is not only marked by the excitement of the Spirit's new and creative possibilities. Like any pilgrimage, it can also lead down paths of potential conflict, danger, and division. That is why it is so important to journey together with one another as we embrace a future yet to be fully revealed, but to be discovered through our commitment to be united with one another, as one body.

---

11. Andrew Walls, "Christianity across Twenty Centuries," in *Atlas of Global Christianity*, p. 48.

CHAPTER THREE

What Divides World Christianity

Endlessly Denominated

The last five hundred years of Christianity have witnessed not only a steady pilgrimage of the faith toward the south and then the east, but also a staggering proliferation of divided institutionalized churches that never could have been imagined in the first fifteen hundred years of Christian history. Protestants call separately organized groups of churches "denominations," meaning specific associations of congregations with distinct beliefs and governance. The term makes no ecclesiological sense to Orthodox or Catholic traditions, which conceive of the church as one entity unified in doctrine and a structure of authority.

Yet, from the Reformation on, Christians in Europe began organizing themselves into separate and distinct groups, sometimes also called "sects." In the democratic cultural and religious soil of the United States, such segmentation flourished. Then, with the modern missionary movement, Christianity was exported with separate and separating identities. Of course, we should not overlook the presence of various non-Western expressions of Christian faith in diverse parts of the world in earlier centuries, such as those from the Orthodox tradition. Particularly in the Middle East, North Africa, and Asia, its ancient churches have maintained their faithful witness through the ages. But on the whole, apart from the Orthodox and Catholic traditions, Christianity began a process of rapid proliferation into groups "denominated" from one another, and that process has continued to the present day, endlessly.

Trying to provide an objective description of our present situation challenges one's ecclesiological imagination. Some people have tried to keep track of the number of Christian denominations in the world. Perhaps no one has devoted more energy in recent decades to this task than David Barrett, whose faithful, continuing research was foundational to the *World Christian Encyclopedia,* with its second edition published in 2001.[1] This impressive resource estimated that Christianity had divided into 33,820 separate denominations by the end of the second millennium. The Center for the Study of Global Christianity at Gordon-Conwell Theological Seminary continues to keep track of these estimates, with help from the Pew Forum. Most recently, they report having obtained information on 41,000 denominations worldwide. A separate website that attempts to explain these numbers, and regularly updates them, has a present estimate of 43,800 denominations, followed by the note, "Please pray for Christian unity."[2]

These estimates are astonishing, and indicate the growing complexity, enormous diversity, and proliferating disunity of world Christianity. Then consider this fact. The World Council of Churches (WCC) has faithfully and courageously carried the vocation of Christian unity for the past sixty years. Yet, it comprises only 349 denominations, or member churches. The changing dynamics of world Christianity are rapidly outpacing the ability of existing structures to comprehend and respond to these new realities.

Thus, the pilgrimage of Christianity, measured since the time when the Gutenberg Bible was printed and then the Reformation that followed a few decades later, has witnessed the continuous and endless fracturing of its organizational life, which has spread around the world. In South Korea alone, for instance, there are about 100 separate Presbyterian denominations. Stories like this abound. Further, when simply analyzing these distressing numbers, the conclusion is that the momentum is in the direction of accelerating institutional fragmentation.

Some would argue that proliferating denominations simply provide endless creativity and unfettered opportunities for Christian groups to find unique identities and appeal to narrow subsets of people. Certainly the contextual adaptation of Christianity requires a continued openness to new forms and expressions of faith. But usually

---

1. David B. Barrett, George Thomas Kurian, and Todd M. Johnson, *World Christian Encyclopedia,* 2nd ed. (Oxford and New York: Oxford University Press, 2001).
2. http://www.philvaz.com/apologetics/a106.htm.

denominational division is motivated by less honorable goals. These endless divisions more often arise out of judgment of fellow Christians, and convictions that separation is required for purity of practice and fidelity of doctrine, even in its most minute specifics. We now have tens of thousands of versions of what such "purity" looks like. The default assumption is that differences are not opportunities for experiencing the diversity of the Holy Spirit's gifts, but rather excuses for dividing — denominating — ourselves from one another.

Even more regrettably, modern denominational divisions are often driven by crass motives of money, power, and pride. Often, new denominations are created simply as ways to exercise control and power by a person or faction, and then justified by some obscure doctrinal rationale. All this makes a mockery of the church's witness. So the existence of more than 40,000 denominations in the world is not only a measure of flagrant disobedience with respect to God's desire for the church; the paths that have led the church to this reality are littered with sin. Our contemporary practice shamelessly violates biblical teachings in ways unimaginable to those who wrote the New Testament and to the leaders of the early church.

Geographically Separated

The movement of Christianity toward the global South and East is altering its centers of authority, influence, and direction. While we normally think of divisions in world Christianity as consisting of doctrinal questions and theological traditions — and those do play a role — the future will be marked as well by divisions that are rooted in geographical realities, reflecting the globe's North-South divide. On many questions, whether voices from the Christian community are from the South or the North may be more determinative of their perspective than whether they are Protestant or Catholic.

The dramatic shift in world Christianity has intensified the divisions and tensions in the global church and its ecumenical institutions. While the massive growth in the Christian family has come in the global South, financial resources and material power remain concentrated in the global North and West. With this comes the continuing, quiet assumption that northern centers of power in the church are still in control and are able to shape the destiny of world Christianity. That assumption, while true in some material ways, is becoming more and more a spiritual and practical illusion.

In this light, consider the geographical location of global Christian institutions. The World Council of Churches, the Lutheran World Federation, and other ecumenical bodies stubbornly cling to their comfortable location at the Ecumenical Centre in Geneva, Switzerland. Geneva is the fifth most expensive city for expatriates in the entire world. The World Communion of Reformed Churches was finally forced to move its offices away from Geneva to save money. But they made a grave mistake by relocating to Hanover, Germany, instead of Johannesburg, South Africa, or another location south of the equator. The Baptist World Alliance is located outside of Washington, D.C., and the World Methodist Council, incredibly enough, has its global center in Lake Junaluska, North Carolina.

The Anglican Communion, of course, is centered in London. World Vision International has its headquarters in California, and the World Evangelical Alliance has its main office in New York. This list could go on, underscoring the practical, visible evidence of geographical divisions and the imbalance of power. The church cannot sustain itself when the center of gravity for global Christianity moves with increasing speed to the global South and East, while the centers of the ecumenical movement and organizations of major evangelical influence remain rooted in the North and the West. It's a formula for intensifying geographical tensions in the global church.

The seismic shift across all of Christianity from the North to the South is presenting a new set of challenges to the unity of the church, within communions, between denominations, and among ecumenical and international organizations. Such geographical divisions are creating serious threats to the oneness and sense of mutual belonging in the body of Christ, seen especially around issues of money, power, international decision making, and intellectual/theological capital.

One can only imagine how Paul and other New Testament voices would challenge the economic, racial, and cultural divisions that have become manifest through the shift of Christianity's center of gravity away from the North and West, and toward the South and East. The task of making manifest the variety of spiritual gifts and backgrounds, rooted in diverse languages and cultures, has become a spiritual imperative in the global church. Bridging the church's geographical divide is a twenty-first-century challenge to all Christians, and essential to becoming one visible people of God.

Spiritually Bifurcated

In the last hundred years, the dramatic geographical pilgrimage of world Christianity was accompanied by the unpredicted advent and eventual eruption of the Pentecostal movement as a powerful force, drastically altering the landscape of the global Christian community. When the Edinburgh World Missionary Conference was held in 1910, the existence of the modern Pentecostal movement was virtually unknown to those who gathered there. A century later, about one out of every four Christians in the world is Pentecostal or charismatic, according to a December 2011 report of the Pew Forum on Religion and Public Life.[3] Along with the story of the growth of the church in Africa, it is hard to name a more critical and formative development in the last century of Christian history.

It is estimated that 80 percent of new conversions in Asia are Pentecostal or charismatic.[4] Almost one in four Pentecostals (23 percent) live in Asia, and nearly one in three (31 percent) are in Africa.[5] What northern liberal and evangelical Christians often fail to recognize is that Pentecostalism comes to the global South without the history and baggage of colonialism. As Douglas Jacobsen says, "In a sense, Pentecostal/ Charismatic Christianity is post-colonial by nature. It encourages local Christian autonomy and cultural adaptation (glocalism) wherever it goes, and that has made it an especially attractive form of faith in the global south."[6]

While distinctions between "Pentecostal," "independent," and other "renewal" churches and movements become complex, the overall trend seems clear. Churches in the Pentecostal tradition and style, with their emphasis on immediate spiritual experiences, detached Christianity from its white missionary control and empowered indigenous expressions of Christian faith within many parts of the world.

The *Atlas of Global Christianity* puts it this way: "Pentecostalism . . . became the main contributor to the reshaping of Christianity from a

3. Pew Forum on Religion and Public Life, "Global Christianity: A Report on the Size and Distribution of the World's Christian Community," December 19, 2011.

4. Todd M. Johnson and Kenneth R. Ross, eds., *Atlas of Global Christianity, 1910-2010* (Edinburgh: Edinburgh University Press, 2009), p. 139.

5. Douglas G. Jacobsen, *The World's Christians: Who They Are, Where They Are, and How They Got There* (London: Wiley-Blackwell, 2011), p. 51.

6. Jacobsen, *The World's Christians,* p. 373.

predominantly Western to a predominantly non-Western phenomenon in the twentieth century."[7]

In Africa, the growth of African "Instituted," or "Independent," Churches, represented by the Organization of African Instituted Churches with its offices in Nairobi, gives further expression to those churches established as independent from the colonial missionary movement and its denominational institutions. These vibrant church communities, often with millions of members, are frequently off the radar of those from the North and West, but are having a deep impact on Christianity within Africa and, through migration, beyond to other regions.

The growth rate in the Pentecostal, charismatic, and renewal movements of Christianity is nearly five times that of the overall growth of global Christianity, dramatically changing its composition and its theological diversity.[8] Rapid growth, as mentioned, has come in Latin America, so that today Brazil has not only the largest number of Catholics of any country, but also the largest number of Pentecostals. Meanwhile, in Asia there are an estimated 873,000 Chinese charismatic congregations.[9]

Combined with this is the overall growth of those Christians who can be classified as "independents," meaning that they are not part of the Catholic, Anglican, Orthodox, or historic Protestant traditions. The growth of such churches has been another defining characteristic of world Christianity, with such Christians now constituting 16 percent of the global Christian community. In Asia, partly because of China, the growth of such independent churches has been especially rapid; today, there are more Christians in such independent churches (142 million) than in the Catholic Church (138 million).[10]

While world Christianity was being radically reshaped by the growth of churches that are Pentecostal and evangelical, as well as other highly indigenous expressions of Christianity especially in the global South, the modern ecumenical movement was also under way. Its achievements have been historic and often extremely remarkable from the time of the Edinburgh World Missionary Conference. Churches of the Ortho-

---

7. Johnson and Ross, *Atlas of Global Christianity,* p. 100.
8. Johnson and Ross, *Atlas of Global Christianity,* p. 102.
9. Johnson and Ross, *Atlas of Global Christianity,* p. 70.
10. Johnson and Ross, *Atlas of Global Christianity,* p. 136.

dox tradition have been brought into sustained fellowship with historic Protestantism through the World Council of Churches. The common witness and theological dialogues at local, national, regional, and global levels have ushered in new realities and reconciled many old and painful divisions between denominations.

Yet, the churches involved in the ecumenical movement, and those churches that are part of the dramatically growing Pentecostal, independent, evangelical, and indigenous churches, have functioned largely in two separate worlds. The theological gulf between these two worlds has widened even as Christianity's center of gravity has continued its journey toward the global South. This divide involves doctrinal issues, but it is also marked by deep differences reflected in the fervent style of spirituality, the less structured and more elastic forms of church polity, and the convictional witness and focus on church growth found in these freshly emerging forms of Christianity over the past century. In my judgment, the gulf between these two worlds now constitutes the most pressing challenge to the unity of the church in the twenty-first century.

Of course, it's true that this theological divide between branches of world Christianity is found within both the global North and South. Further, the Catholic Church as one unified global expression of the Christian tradition constitutes another largely separate reality, with its own geographical tensions and dynamics. Nevertheless, the following generalizations can still be helpful.

The churches whose modern historical home and predominant presence have been in the global North carry the *tradition* of the faith and believe in the *catholicity,* or essential unity, of the church. These include churches of the historic Protestant family, the Orthodox family, and the Catholic family as well, given its center in Rome. In their various expressions, these families root Christian faith in ancient creeds and, through understandings of ministry, in the tradition of the church, from its founding. Further, all believe in "one holy, universal catholic (Christian) church." The historic Protestant and Orthodox churches have been the primary members of the WCC and other conciliar ecumenical bodies throughout the world, and the Catholic Church has joined many national councils of churches and participated in other ecumenical expressions.

At the same time, these churches are often struggling to maintain vital and growing ministry within the cultural contexts of the global

North. Patterns of secularization deeply shape European societies, and in the United States, surveys classifying the population according to religion record the fastest growing group as those who reply "no religious affiliation," which is now at 20 percent, and 33 percent for those under thirty.[11] A pattern of overall decline — with some exceptions, of course — tends to characterize these church families in the global North.

Meanwhile, churches in the global South, with their exuberant spirituality and tenacious witness, are propelling the growth of world Christianity. In movements that are like modern revivals, highly creative, indigenous expressions of Christian faith have gained wide adherence. But these churches face their own dangers. Many are highly sectarian. They divide themselves from other expressions of Christianity and often function over against those from other Christian traditions, or even those from other tribes or cultural groups. Rarely is there any commitment to the church "catholic" — meaning the one, broad, universal church. Participation in any ecumenical bodies is rare.

Further, these churches seem easily vulnerable to beliefs and practices that go beyond the boundaries of Christian orthodoxy. Of course, the immediate question they raise is, who is qualified to define the content of such orthodoxy? But indigenous expressions of Christianity founded by highly charismatic, authoritative leaders can lead to beliefs and practices deemed heretical by those who claim their roots in the historical tradition of the church.

It is this theological, cultural, and spiritual divide, reflected in many ways between the churches of the global North and those of the global South, that presents the most fundamental challenge to any hope of Christian unity, and cries out for the attention of all who would follow the words of Ephesians 4: "There is one body and one Spirit, just as you were called to the one hope of your calling, one Lord, one faith, one baptism, one God and Father of all, who is above all and through all and in all" (4:4-6).[12]

The spiritually fervent churches of the global South need the enrichment of the commitment to the tradition and catholicity of Christian faith carried by churches rooted in the global North. And those

---

11. Pew Forum on Religion and Public Life, "'Nones' on the Rise," October 9, 2012: http://www.pewforum.org/Unaffiliated/nones-on-the-rise.aspx.

12. Unless otherwise indicated, all Scripture quotations in this book come from the New Revised Standard Version.

churches need the enrichment of brothers and sisters in the global South who are discovering fresh and vital pathways for participating in God's mission in the world. Building that bridge is the critical global calling today in concretely expressing the unity of the global church.

Institutionally Insulated

The Twenty-third Pentecostal World Conference takes place in Kuala Lumpur, Malaysia, in August 2013. This global gathering is sponsored by the Pentecostal World Fellowship, whose chairman is Dr. Prince Guneratnum, pastor of Calvary Church in Kuala Lumpur. The primary work of this fellowship is sponsoring its world conference, which last took place in Stockholm in 2010, when 2,000 Pentecostal leaders from around the world gathered together.

A few months after the Pentecostal gathering in Kuala Lumpur, the World Council of Churches' Tenth Assembly in Busan, Korea, will gather delegates from every member church for a meeting of the WCC's highest and most important governing body. As many visitors as delegates often attend the WCC assemblies, and these global gatherings of 2,000-3,000 from churches around the world make this a primary event every seven years for shaping and strengthening the ecumenical movement.

A year later, in October 2014, the World Evangelical Alliance (WEA) will hold its General Assembly in Seoul, Korea. In the words of Geoff Tunnicliffe, WEA's general secretary, "Thousands of WEA leaders from around the world will gather to receive a fresh vision on how as followers of Christ, through the empowerment of the Holy Spirit we can see the world impacted through God's transforming power."

This sequence of global Christian gatherings all held in Asia in a span of about fifteen months illustrates dramatically the institutional isolation facing world Christianity. While some overlap will occur between the Pentecostal World Conference and the WEA General Assembly, only a handful of those present at either of these two assemblies will attend the WCC Assembly, and vice versa. The separate worlds in which world Christianity lives are reinforced institutionally.

This institutional partition continues at the regional, national, and local levels. One of the major achievements of the ecumenical movement is the creation of a whole infrastructure of ecumenical organizations, councils, and agencies that function throughout the world. At the time of the Edinburgh Missionary Conference in 1910, only two national councils of churches existed. By 2005, sixty-four national councils had a formal relationship as "associated councils" with the WCC. Many others were also active, and often sponsored affiliated agencies. The ACT Alliance, created in 2010 out of initiatives from the WCC, brings together 130 church-related organizations worldwide working together in development, humanitarian assistance, and advocacy around issues of justice, peace, care for creation, human rights, HIV/AIDS, and similar concerns.

Regional ecumenical organizations also function throughout the world, again often linked to various programmatic initiatives addressing a similar agenda of issues as part of their common Christian witness. And at the global level, a number of Christian world communions play a role. These function on a worldwide level, attempting to draw together those from specific Christian traditions, such as the Lutheran World Federation, the World Communion of Reformed Churches, the World Methodist Council, the Baptist World Alliance, the Mennonite World Conference, and many more.

This maze of often overlapping ecumenical organizations, many of which rely heavily for funding on a relatively small group of agencies and churches in the global North, was analyzed in a major study for the WCC done by Jill Hawkey in 2005, titled *Mapping the Oikoumene.*[13] It's the single best resource I'm aware of that describes the complex ecumenical infrastructure that was mostly established in the second half of the twentieth century.

However, in nearly a parallel universe, a worldwide infrastructure of more evangelically oriented global institutions, mission organizations, relief and development agencies, and advocacy groups working on a similar agenda of issues (justice, peace, care of creation, human rights, HIV/AIDS, etc.), along with national associations, functions energetically. The Micah Network, for instance, links together 532 evangelically based organizations, nongovernmental organizations, local community development groups, and others around the world in activities including community development, gender equity, and HIV/AIDS, focused around an understanding of "integral mission." The Micah Challenge is a global advocacy effort aimed at holding governments ac-

---

13. Jill Hawkey, *Mapping the Oikoumene: A Study of Current Ecumenical Structures and Relationships* (Geneva: World Council of Churches, 2005).

countable to the U.N.'s Millennium Development Goals, and ending extreme poverty by 2015.

The World Evangelical Alliance provides a global network attempting to link together the parts of this evangelical infrastructure. Its complex membership structure includes 129 national evangelical alliances, various Global Partners (the Micah Network falls into this category), about 100 evangelical organizations called "associates," and various denominations. An evangelical statement of faith provides a common theological basis, and its mission statement reads as follows: "World Evangelical Alliance exists to foster Christian unity and to provide a worldwide identity, voice and platform to Evangelical Christians. Seeking empowerment by the Holy Spirit, they extend the Kingdom of God by proclamation of the Gospel to all nations and by Christ-centered transformation within society."[14]

WEA's activities include initiatives on religious freedom, nuclear weapons, human trafficking, and creation care, among others. The Alliance claims to give a voice and platform to 600 million Christians worldwide. In comparable fashion the WCC represents 560 million Christians in 110 countries. These largely equal groups function in two separate, institutionally insulated worlds.

Then, of course, the Catholic Church functions globally with its own massive network of churches, orders, associations, and institutions, comprising about half of all the Christians in the world. The Vatican has steadfastly declined to become a full member of the WCC. Instead, it participates in a "Joint Working Group." However, the councils of bishops in many countries have agreed to join national councils of churches. Further, following Vatican II, the Pontifical Council for Promoting Christian Unity established bilateral dialogues with a wide range of other Christian communions and traditions.

Yet, while generalizations are nearly impossible, it's fair to say that Catholicism's structures of authority, with its more recent, conservatively oriented appointments of bishops, work to maintain a cohesive presence that is largely institutionally insulated from the other major streams of Christianity.

To this picture we can add the Orthodox churches. Almost all of these participate in the World Council of Churches and other ecumenical bodies. That has been an ecumenical achievement of major significance,

---

14. From the WEA website, http://www.worldea.org/whoweare/vision-mission.

which is often overlooked. Yet, in their own contexts the Orthodox churches are usually a tightly knit, culturally and ethnically connected ecclesial reality with a strong self-understanding of constituting the one undivided church.

So here's the present story. The divisions within the worldwide body of Christ are continually reinforced, on a daily basis, through institutional power at local, national, regional, and global levels that keep the vast majority of Christians, congregations, denominations, and organizations functioning within their separate worlds, isolated from the other major expressions of world Christianity. The irony is that the ecumenical movement, despite its significant accomplishments, functions often as one of those isolated worlds.

Certainly voices will quickly say that things are better, and progress is being made. Denominational barriers are breaking down. Evangelicals and Pentecostals are more open to relationships with others. New and recent interchanges have taken root between the WCC and the World Pentecostal Fellowship. The Catholic Church has been changing since Vatican II. And so on. All those things are true. But in reality, there are so few places, such a lack of resources, so few organizations, and such a weak infrastructure for nurturing and strengthening the unity that must break down these massive institutionalized worlds that keep us so comfortably, and so sinfully, separated from one another. The truth is that most of the world's Christians function in separate worlds of ecclesiological apartheid — Catholic, historic Protestant, evangelical/Pentecostal, and Orthodox.

The only way to bridge these major geographical, theological, and institutional divides permeating world Christianity is to establish a safe space in which those representing the full breadth of the global Christian community can gather. Fragile steps to do so have been taken through initiatives like the Global Christian Forum, but they confront the reality of deeply entrenched institutional insularity.

Generational Isolation

The denominational, geographical, spiritual, and institutional divides that separate the *koinonia* of world Christianity must be addressed and eventually overcome. No call to Christian unity is credible today if it fails to confront each of these challenges. But beyond these, it seems to me, is a major generational rift that impedes all our efforts to experience the unity of the church. As the world has watched sweeping political and social changes being driven by young adults and spread by the communication tools that have been embedded into their subcultures, it's essential to ask what this means for the future of world Christianity.

In my understanding, our contemporary generational divide is qualitatively different from the normal tension between younger people and their elders. Today's youth and younger adults approach the world, with its patterns of organizational structure, in fundamentally different ways. The tools of social networking are the means through which flexible groups of relationships provide meaning, value, and belonging in one's life. Moreover, the incredible and immediate access to information available at one's fingertips undermines the role that institutions and authority structures traditionally have played as sources of reliable truth and guidance.

These features affect participation in the church as well. This emerging generation is less concerned about dogma and more focused on authentic spirituality. Membership and loyalty to religious institutions — including ecumenical organizations of all kinds — are seriously eroding, but the quest for transcendent reality, and the thirst for more immediate spiritual communities, seems to grow.

A major, five-year research project headed by David Kinnaman, president of the Barna Group, found that nearly 60 percent of young adults in the United States who regularly attended church detached themselves from church life either permanently or for long periods after age fifteen. Among the reasons given were that "churches seem overly protective" and that the young adults' "experience of Christianity is shallow."[15] When I visited South Korea in 2012 and asked why the earlier growth of the church in that country had seriously stagnated, pastors related to me the widespread loss of interest and participation by young people.

Ecumenical organizations and denominations all try earnestly to get more young people involved in their institutional life. Many establish, and even fight over, quotas for the representation of youth at their governing bodies. Rules are relaxed and initiatives are taken to get young people into rooms filled with gray-haired veterans earnestly concerned about the future of these institutions.

---

15. See http://www.barna.org/teens-next-gen-articles/528-six-reasons-young-christians-leave-church.

But what if this younger generation simply doesn't feel at home within these expressions of organizational life? Moreover, what if they are convinced that there are far more effective ways of carrying out these desired goals and purposes? What if we are spending too much energy trying to fit a younger generation into predetermined patterns of institutional life, and not enough time listening to how their wisdom and journeys might lead us down new pathways toward the values that we all cherish?

Why do church leaders struggle to convince young people to participate in our church or ecumenical gatherings while the Taizé community in France, and its expressions elsewhere in the world, draws thousands of young adults to gather, camp out, worship, and experience a community together? And this, of course, was not even Taizé's purpose when it was founded.

My conviction, based on experience in the North American context, is that we must come to understand the church less as an organization and more as an organism, if we are to engage this emerging generation. They are turned off by religion, yet they can become fascinated with the person of Jesus and the radical, countercultural way of life he offers. They reject versions of Christianity that are captive to political ideologies, but desire integrity to be demonstrated, where words about justice and reconciliation are clearly reflected in actions.

We can only begin to imagine what this means for the quest for the unity of the people of God in the changing context of world Christianity. One unanswered question is whether the attitudes discovered among church-related young adults in the United States are similar to those of young adults in the global South regarding established religious institutions, or whether significant differences exist. Can a globalized youth culture bridge the North-South divide in world Christianity, or not?

We should learn to foster creative methods that invite younger generations of Christians, from all the diverse regions and expressions of the church, to connect directly in ways of their own creation, not mediated by our present maze of denominational, organizational, and ecumenical structures. Someone needs to create Faithbook.

Perhaps new models of global *koinonia* might emerge, and even acquire a revolutionary momentum that could open creative ways to bridge the divisions afflicting the global body of Christ. If events once thought unimaginable and driven by a younger generation could suddenly create dramatic political and social changes in whole countries in the Arab world, why would we not believe that equally dramatic changes that overcome the divisions in world Christianity could happen in the life of our churches?

Conclusion

The inspiring pilgrimage of world Christianity is accompanied by stark and serious challenges that divide and fracture the body of Christ. On a global level, Christianity is becoming endlessly denominated, geographically separated, spiritually bifurcated, institutionally insulated, and generationally isolated. It will take a sustained and courageous commitment by Christians, including those in leadership in congregations, denominations, and organizations around the world, to find our way toward rediscovering and making visible the Spirit's gift of unity.

Doing so, however, requires an understanding of why this quest is important, or even necessary, in the life of world Christianity. That drives us back to explore foundational biblical perspectives regarding God's intentions for those who live as members of Christ's body, the church. Proof texts or ecumenical slogans won't suffice. The depth of divisions within world Christianity, presenting a new and daunting agenda, requires a commensurate and probing exploration of whether and why, according to the biblical witness, these should be addressed, and overcome. That is where we shall now turn our attention.

CHAPTER FOUR

God's Heart for Unity

Pilgrims came from every part of the dusty land, walking with families, often for days. They were heading for the place that celebrated the heart of their faith, where their first king began his reign, and where a magnificent temple was host to the special, holy presence of their God. This pilgrim journey always led them upward, for this city, revered by all their people, was set upon a hill. They were making a holy pilgrimage to Jerusalem.

Three times a year, special religious festivals became occasions when faithful Jews could make such a pilgrimage — the Feast of Unleavened Bread (Passover), the Feast of Harvest (Pentecost), and the Feast of Ingathering (Tabernacles) (Leviticus 23:2; Exodus 23:14-15). And as they traveled, they would remember and recite the promises of their God. Meeting with other pilgrims from different tribes and parts of their land, they joined together in their journey. These times of pilgrimage and religious celebration expressed their unity as a people of God.

Thankfully, the memory of what these pilgrims sang, recited, and recounted to one another is partially preserved. They are the Psalms of Ascent, fifteen precious expressions of this journey into God's presence, Psalms 120 to 134. Most biblical scholars agree that these words of Scripture have their roots in the pilgrimage and the gathering together of the people of Israel at these special times of worship and celebration.

A key and inspiring part of this pilgrimage, culminating at the temple in Jerusalem, was the experience of the unity of the children of Israel. Psalm 133 sings the blessedness of this unity:

How very good and pleasant it is
    when kindred live together in unity!
It is like the precious oil on the head,
    running down upon the beard,
on the beard of Aaron,
    running down over the collar of his robes.
It is like the dew of Hermon,
    which falls on the mountains of Zion.
For there the LORD ordained his blessing,
    life forevermore. (vv. 1-3)

This came, of course, out of the existential experience of the children of Israel, who experienced division between the northern kingdom and Judah. In fact, in 2 Chronicles 30 King Hezekiah reestablished the Feast of the Passover for all Israel, reaching out to the remnant remaining in the northern kingdom after it had been conquered by Assyria as well as throughout Judah, sending couriers inviting all to join in the celebration in Jerusalem. Calling people to make a pilgrimage to Jerusalem for this feast was a move to restore the unity of the people of Israel. And so we read: "The whole assembly of Judah, the priests and the Levites, and the whole assembly that came out of Israel, and the resident aliens who came out of the land of Israel, and the resident aliens who lived in Judah, rejoiced. There was great joy in Jerusalem, for since the time of Solomon son of King David of Israel there had been nothing like this in Jerusalem" (2 Chronicles 30:25-26).

We can imagine, then, what it meant for pilgrims going to Jerusalem, throughout Israel's history, to sing, "How very good and pleasant it is when kindred live together in unity." In the time of their exile, as the people of Israel hoped for their return and restoration, Jerusalem was a symbol of their unity as a people. And with Joseph and Mary, Jesus made this same pilgrimage, traveling from Nazareth up to Jerusalem for the Festival of the Passover, maybe every year. Luke records one journey when he was twelve (Luke 2:41-51). It's likely that Jesus joined with others in singing the Psalms of Ascent and celebrating the unity of God's people.

Our Present Setting

This image of the children of Israel on a pilgrimage to Jerusalem under-scores God's heart for the unity of God's people. This yearning is embedded deep within the biblical story, long before the birth of Jesus. Today we tend to regard the quest for Christian unity as a project. It is undertaken mostly by hundreds of ecumenical bodies on the global, regional, national, and local levels, as well as by confessional families. Often these organizations actually find themselves in conflict with other Christian churches and groups.

Meanwhile, world Christianity is faced with the severe and challenging divisions that have been described. We live in a sinful sea of proliferating denominations, accompanied by acrimonious conflicts, theological witch hunts, legal conflicts, and self-righteous judgments. The pervasive divisions of all types in the body of Christ today are not just a disgrace. Rather, they stand, I believe, under God's harsh judgment for they strike against the very character of God.

No remedy will come simply through encouraging Christians and churches to shore up the crumbling infrastructure of ecumenical organizations. Our problem, and indeed our sin, is much deeper. Our repentance requires, first of all, an acknowledgment of how deeply we find ourselves trapped in sinful disobedience. This means recovering and restoring in depth the biblical story, and the roots of our calling to belong together as one body.

But repentance does not simply mean confessing our sin. The word *metanoia* means "turning around" and walking in a new direction. So we need to explore what the pilgrimage of God's people toward places of unity, worship, witness, service, and celebration would look like today. It's essential that we discover new paths to guide this journey.

Beginning in Jerusalem

The biblical call to unity continues in the New Testament. The church was born on the Day of Pentecost, when Jerusalem was filled with pilgrims. The disciples and followers "were all together in one place" (Acts 2:1), probably to pray and recite Hebrew Scripture, as was the customary practice at this feast.

The dramatic outpouring and filling of the Holy Spirit was immediately made manifest in the astonishing unity that was created. "Devout Jews from every nation under heaven" (Acts 2:5) heard the disciples speak about God's deeds of power in their own languages (2:6-12). God's Holy Spirit overcame these divisions, beginning to create a new, unified people, who responded to the message and evidence of God's power, and repented, believed, and were called into the body of Christ.

The first descriptions of this body — the genesis of the church — are ones of profound, and even startling, unity and interdependence. This is an initial portrayal of the church: "Awe came upon everyone, because many wonders and signs were being done by the apostles. All who believed were together and had all things in common; they would sell their possessions and goods and distribute the proceeds to all, as any had need. Day by day, as they spent much time together in the temple, they broke bread at home and ate their food with glad and generous hearts, praising God and having the goodwill of all the people. And day by day the Lord added to their number those who were being saved" (Acts 2:43-47).

This was not simply a unity of belief, or even a unity of liturgical practice. It was a unity of life. God's Spirit formed the church as a community, living together as one people, in Jerusalem. This was a dramatic fulfillment, at a whole new level, of the hopes and prayers of pilgrims who had journeyed over the centuries to this holy city.

Unity Tested by Mission

This foundational unity of the early, emerging church was tested by its mission. While the Great Commission was given to the disciples at the Mount of Olives near Jerusalem (Acts 1:8-12; Matthew 28:16-20, although this later reference places these words in Galilee), the missional outreach of the early church had its roots not in Jerusalem, but in Antioch.

Persecution faced these first believers in Jerusalem. The high priest had the apostles arrested and ordered them, unsuccessfully, to stop preaching. Then Stephen was arrested and stoned to death, while Saul looked on with approval.

Many of these early followers of Jesus fled Jerusalem, and some traveled as far as Antioch (Acts 8:4; 11:19). That was 300 miles away, a journey taking about ten days on foot. Antioch was not only separated geographically from Jerusalem. Culturally, socially, politically, and religiously, it was a different world.

Antioch was the third largest city in the Roman Empire, after Rome and Alexandria, with up to 500,000 inhabitants. In stark contrast to Jerusalem, and its Palestinian Judaism, Antioch was a city of Hellenistic culture, including its various deities and religious practices.

It was here, in Antioch, that the gospel, brought by those fleeing Jerusalem, took root and flourished. The story is described in the eleventh chapter of Acts. The gospel was shared with Greeks, and many came to faith as this young church grew. The startling and radical assertion was that one did not have to enter into the grace of God in Christ through Jewish identity or practices. This fellowship was not dependent upon continuing observance of Jewish law or worship in the synagogue, but solely upon embracing the message of Jesus, and acknowledging him as the Christ, and Lord.

So the amazing, incarnational power of the gospel of Jesus Christ, the word that was made flesh in the Jewish culture just outside Jerusalem, in the city of David, now became incarnate within this foreign, cosmopolitan Greek culture of one of the empire's leading cities. Christian faith defined its identity through making this first, formative journey from Jewish to Greek culture. And the church at Antioch became the crucible for the missional imagination of the early church.

We know the conflict that followed, as recorded in Acts. The church in Jerusalem — those apostles and others who survived and maintained a presence as the "headquarters" of the church — was unsettled. It sent Barnabas to Antioch to investigate how the gospel could be shared with non-Jews, and how Jewish practices could be discarded. "When he came and saw the grace of God, he rejoiced, and he exhorted them all to remain faithful to the Lord with steadfast devotion" (Acts 11:23). Many more believed, and the church continued to grow.

The conflict wasn't resolved until the Council of Jerusalem met, recorded in Acts 15. Those in Antioch respected the reasonable requests from the founding church in Jerusalem. Upon listening to the experience of what God's grace was doing, the church in Jerusalem affirmed and empowered the fresh expression of the gospel in Antioch. Thus, the church in Antioch became the first "missional church" and the center of the early church's mission in the world, sending Paul and Barnabas to Cyprus and beyond.

At the heart of this biblical story is the lesson that the church's most serious conflict — the relationship between Gentiles and Jews — was resolved through an underlying, spiritually empowered commitment to be one body, unified, and together. Differences were respected and reconciled in discerning ways, with honest and earnest dialogue, motivated by the question we can well imagine Barnabas asking, "What is the Spirit doing here?" This first "ecumenical council" in Acts 15 modeled how the church is to live together, with cultural diversity, theological differences, and richness of the Spirit's various gifts, building and maintaining the unity of the body in its ongoing work and mission.

Made to Drink of One Spirit

Of course, conflict in the early church was not solved by the Council of Jerusalem. Far from it. But the most striking features in the biblical story of the early church are not the ongoing accounts of strife, but rather the persistent ministry of Paul and the apostles to strengthen and build the unity of this growing, missionary church. The exhortations, admonitions, examples, metaphors, and instructions about how the body of Christ is to live together as one interdependent, unified community, reconciling vast differences, permeate the New Testament.

First Corinthians, for example, is one of the earliest books in the New Testament, probably written around A.D. 54 from Ephesus, toward the start of Paul's second missionary journey. Here, Paul uses the metaphor of the human body to describe the church (1 Corinthians 12:12-31). It's inconceivable, obviously, that any part of the human body severed from the rest has any life or function. The body functions only because each part belongs to the whole, dependent upon one another.

The verses that introduce this metaphor are particularly striking: "For just as the body is one and has many members, and all the members of the body, though many, are one body, so it is with Christ. For in the one Spirit we were all baptized into one body — Jews or Greeks, slaves or free — and we were all made to drink of one Spirit" (12:12-13).

This constitutes, in my view, one of the most prescient passages of Scripture speaking to the unity of the church. Notice, we have no choice in this matter. All of us have been baptized into one body. So we all have been *made to drink of one Spirit.* That is the starting point, the reality. Our challenge is to live with one another in the church from the basis of this truth.

Clearly, Paul is not thinking about just those in the church at Corinth. When he says "all," he means all who are part of the body of Christ, everywhere. The image of the body and the interdependence of its members, which follows in verses 14-31, applies to the church universal. This is also shown by his listing of gifts and roles, in verse 28: "God has appointed in the church first apostles, second prophets, third teachers; then deeds of power, then gifts of healing, forms of assistance, forms of leadership. . . ."

This powerful metaphor of the human body for picturing how the church lives in unity is preceded at the start of the chapter with a description of the varieties of spiritual gifts, all given by the same Spirit, for the common good (12:4-11). He returns to this thought at the end of chapter 12, describing these various gifts that function in the body, and urging all to "strive for the greater gifts" (12:31).

This is how Paul introduces the famous words found in 1 Corinthians 13 on the character and preeminent importance of love. The words of this chapter are treasured and inspiring, including these verses: "Love is patient; love is kind; love is not envious or boastful or arrogant or rude. It does not insist on its own way; it is not irritable or resentful; it does not rejoice in wrongdoing, but rejoices in the truth. It bears all things, believes all things, hopes all things, endures all things. Love never ends" (13:4-8).

Of course, this chapter is frequently read at weddings to celebrate the love between a husband and a wife. But nothing could have been further from Paul's mind.

These words culminate all that Paul has been saying about how all those in the church are to live and work together with one another. Being one body, and knowing we have all been "made to drink of one Spirit" while exercising different gifts, is possible only by striving for and exercising the gift of love described here.

These aren't the only places in 1 Corinthians where the call to unity in the body is addressed. Right after its opening greeting and thanksgiving, the epistle addresses the challenge: "Now I appeal to you, brothers and sisters, by the name of our Lord Jesus Christ, that all of you be in agreement and that there be no divisions among you, but that you be united in the same mind and the same purpose. For it has been reported to me by Chloe's people that there are quarrels among you, my brothers and sisters. What I mean is that each of you says, 'I belong to Paul,' or 'I belong to Apollos,' or 'I belong to Cephas,' or 'I belong to Christ.' Has Christ been divided?" (1:10-13).

Paul's strong words are meant to condemn any idea of separate identities or factions, based on important leaders, within the life of the church. But that's a practice that we take for granted today. We identify ourselves as followers of Calvin, Luther, Wesley . . . the list goes on and on. Pentecostal and evangelical megachurches, especially with televised ministries, revolve around the life of their founding leader. Some churches in the African Instituted Churches elevate the role of their founder or leader to exalted spiritual heights, such as the Prophet Simon Kimbangu, founder of the Church of Jesus Christ of the Prophet Simon Kimbangu.

The Corinthian passages that obviously are taken from the early liturgy of the Lord's Supper, and that we repeat in its celebration today, contain more striking admonitions to unity: "The bread that we break, is it not a sharing in the body of Christ? Because there is one bread, we who are many are one body, for we all partake of the one bread" (10:16b-17).

A few verses later, in chapter 11, when the familiar words of institution of the Lord's Supper are recounted, they come directly in response to reports, cited in the preceding verses, of divisions and factions in the church. For Paul, this is a violation of the church's identity, and contradicts the worship and practice of the Lord's Supper at the heart of its life.

With All the Saints

Equally powerful calls to the church's identity and unity as one people called by God are found in the epistle to the Ephesians. These words were written later than the Corinthian letters, perhaps by Paul when he was imprisoned in Rome, shortly before his death, although New Testament scholars have a variety of theories about both its authorship and date.

Years ago in my Christian journey, I was a member of Church of the Saviour in Washington, D.C. This experimental congregation was started by Gordon Cosby, and Elizabeth O'Conner wrote several books about its life. The long process of becoming a member in this church ends when one's "spiritual autobiography" is shared with the church council, and one is then received as a new member during a Sunday service. At that time, the new member chooses a particular passage of Scripture that has become central to his or her journey. I chose Ephesians 3:14-19:

For this reason I bow my knees before the Father, from whom every family in heaven and on earth takes its name. I pray that, according to the riches of his glory, he may grant that you may be strengthened in your inner being with power through his Spirit, and that Christ may dwell in your hearts through faith, as you are being rooted and grounded in love. I pray that you may have the power to comprehend, with all the saints, what is the breadth and length and height and depth, and to know the love of Christ that surpasses knowledge, so that you may be filled with all the fullness of God.

In the four decades since that time, I've continued to find that passage compelling, informing work for the unity of the body of Christ. These words underscore that the ability to truly comprehend, even "beyond knowledge," the extent of the love of Christ depends upon seeking this *"with all the saints."*

Certainly that's been true in my experience, as it has for many others. As one in the Reformed tradition, my ecumenical encounters through the years with Orthodox theologians, Catholic contemplative monks, Pentecostal leaders, evangelical preachers, Anabaptist authors, Lutheran bishops, Anglican priests, and charismatic pastors from African Instituted Churches have all revealed to me, in ways I never would otherwise have grasped, the *"breadth and length and height and depth"* of the love of Christ.

The New Testament scholar Markus Barth, in his commentary on Ephesians in the Anchor Bible series, shares this clarifying truth about the passage: "The reference to 'all saints' in 3:18 points out a consequence: either worship, theological work, and spiritual insight are ecumenical events or they have nothing to do with the knowledge and proclamation of God."[1]

The epistle's powerful call to unity continues into the fourth chapter, where the author frames this as a matter central to following our basic call from God: "I therefore, the prisoner in the Lord, beg you to lead a life worthy of the calling to which you have been called, with all humility and gentleness, with patience, bearing with one another in love, making every effort to maintain the unity of the Spirit in the bond of peace. There is one body and one Spirit, just as you were called to the

---

1. Markus Barth, *Ephesians*, Anchor Bible (Garden City, N.Y.: Doubleday, 1974), p. 395.

one hope of your calling, one Lord, one faith, one baptism, one God and Father of all, who is above all and through all and in all" (4:1-6).

We can think of this passage, and the verses that follow dealing with the variety of spiritual gifts (4:7-16), almost like a constitution of the church. It describes how we are to live together, in light of the confession of what we believe together. Our calling to live this way does not come from Paul, but from God, and the qualities of love in 1 Corinthians 13 are echoed here.

Most important, we are not called to create unity in the body of Christ. I don't think that formulation is ever found in the New Testament. Rather, we are to *"maintain the unity of the Spirit."* This unity already exists. It is the underlying foundation. The unity of the body of Christ is not a project to be undertaken; it is a promised reality to be realized. As John Howard Yoder has written, "Christian unity is not to be created, but to be obeyed."[2]

We may think of this as we do of salvation. We know that salvation is not something we can achieve through our own work, but a gift we accept as God's grace. But once entering into this new reality, our lives and actions are radically transformed. So it is with the unity of the body of Christ.

Maintaining this unity requires hard, strenuous, and active effort, grounded in internalizing the nature and extent of God's love. The plea is that we make "every effort" to maintain, nurture, and build upon this unity given by the Spirit, doing so "in the bond of peace." Why? Because this is the reality: there is "one body and one Spirit . . . one Lord, one faith, one baptism." We have no other choice.

These biblical themes resonate throughout the New Testament. Instructions to "bear one another's burdens" are also found in Galatians 6:2, explaining that this is how we "fulfill the law of Christ." Such a comparison between how we should act toward one another in light of the unity of the body, and how Christ acted in the pouring out of his life in love, is most dramatic in the second chapter of Philippians: "If then there is any encouragement in Christ, any consolation from love, any sharing in the Spirit, any compassion and sympathy, make my joy complete: be of the same mind, having the same love, being in full accord and of one mind. Do nothing from selfish ambition or conceit, but in

---

2. John Howard Yoder, *The Ecumenical Movement and the Faithful Church* (Scottdale, Pa.: Herald Press, 1958), p. 21.

humility regard others as better than yourselves. Let each of you look not to your own interests, but to the interests of others. Let the same mind be in you that was in Christ Jesus" (Philippians 2:1-5).

What follows, of course, is the hymn of Christ's self-emptying and obedience unto death, and God's exaltation of him as the name above all names. But this example of Christ comes to inspire and encourage his followers to *"be of the same mind, having the same love, being in full accord and of one mind."*

That They May Be One

The verse that most quickly comes to mind when Christians consider the call to the church's unity is from the prayer of Jesus in the seventeenth chapter of the Gospel of John, specifically these verses:

> "I ask not only on behalf of these, but also on behalf of those who will believe in me through their word, that they may all be one. As you, Father, are in me and I am in you, may they also be in us, so that the world may believe that you have sent me. The glory that you have given me I have given them, so that they may be one, as we are one, I in them and you in me, that they may become completely one, so that the world may know that you have sent me and have loved them even as you have loved me." (John 17:20-23)

The passage, and particularly part of verse 21, *"that they may all be one,"* has functioned like an ecumenical proof text. It's quickly cited to prove a point, or begin a presentation, the way other verses become convenient slogans to make various arguments by different Christian groups. In the process, however, we neglect not only the rich context of this particular passage, but we pay little or no attention to the pervasive biblical passages and themes that point to the unity of God's people.

The call to live together from the reality of our oneness in Christ is not derived from any proof text. It's central to the biblical story. This passage from John, however, illumines a further theological understanding of the nature of the church's unity.

The powerful message of these verses is that the oneness of those who believe in Jesus is rooted in the relationship of the Father and the Son. In other words, our unity is founded in the life of the Trinity. The belonging together of those in the body of Christ is made possible by, and infused with the same love that is shared between Jesus and his Father.

Here again, we understand that the unity of believers is a reality that comes from God. Yet, we must courageously embrace this oneness for it to become complete. Doing so, however, is not simply a mystical experience that is only understood "spiritually."

Having been raised in a strong evangelical church, I recall well discussions about how we were "spiritually united" with all who accepted Christ as the Lord and Savior. With such believers, anywhere, we could sense a belonging together; this was the secret, and the meaning of any Christian unity. It didn't really involve the congregation. My home church as a child proudly proclaimed on its bulletin that it was "independent and nondenominational."

I remember well a conversation about this with my college chaplain at Hope College. You can't just talk about some ethereal, spiritual sense of being the church, he told me. The body of Christ has to take on flesh. It has to be somewhere, on a corner, in a place, made of real people, living together as a community, in relationships with one another.

My chaplain's perspectives are reflected in this passage from John. We see both the vertical and the horizontal dimensions of what it means to be living as one body. The union of love between God and the ones who believe is essential. But those so united to God are also united to one another, bound together in a community of love. And for John's Gospel, this is not some spiritual experience; it is practical and real. It takes on flesh. Thus, Christ's prayer that those who believe might be one, just as he and the Father are one, yearns for practical, concrete expression.

This is underscored by the expectation in Christ's prayer that this oneness must be convincing enough to be seen so it can call others to believe. The New Testament scholar Raymond Brown, who has done pioneering work on the Gospel of John, expresses it this way: "Some type of vital, organic unity seems to be demanded by the fact that the relationship of Father and Son is held up as the model of unity. . . . The fact that this unity has to be visible enough to challenge the world to believe seems to militate against a purely spiritual union."[3]

---

3. Raymond Brown, *The Gospel according to John,* Anchor Bible (Garden City, N.Y.: Doubleday, 1970), p. 776.

When evangelicals and other Protestants speak about the unity of the "invisible church," it's well to listen to voices from the Orthodox Church. Consider, for instance, a blog from an Orthodox priest, Michael Reagan, who wrote this:

> "But it is only *the visible church* which is divided," others will claim. "The invisible church, the real Body of Christ, made up of all true believers regardless of denomination, is undivided." Oh please! To which "church" was Christ referring when He said that by its unity men would know it was of Him? Can men see an invisible church? Obviously He was speaking of a visible Church. And can you imagine a definition of the church as "the body of all true believers, regardless of denomination" flying with any of the apostles? Can we picture the Corinthians explaining to Paul that they weren't really divided; they were all simply members of the "invisible church" who merely couldn't agree on a few "non-essentials"?[4]

Those of us in the Protestant, evangelical, and Pentecostal traditions have to become far more honest in dealing with the biblical imperatives calling us to live out of the basis of the unity of the body of Christ, given by God and empowered by the Holy Spirit. In the Reformed tradition, there is a healthy view that the "true church" is beyond one's own denominational boundaries. That, of course, is an ecumenically essential conviction. It should serve as a powerful motivation to seek to build further bonds of fellowship and nurture our unity in concrete ways.

But sometimes the idea of a "spiritual unity" is used to ignore, discount, or disregard the concrete divisions severing the life of Christ's body. It's biblically irresponsible and theologically suspect to hide behind notions of an "invisible unity" as a way to shield ourselves from the striking disobedience and sin of divisions in the church today. Such a weak and, I would say, docetic ecclesiology conveniently blinds us from our own responsibility for disobeying the words of Scripture.

These issues are being played out in the dramatic search for real and visible unity among churches of the Reformed tradition in South Africa, divided so cruelly and tragically by race. In the midst of the strug-

---

4. Father Michael Reagan, "Christian Unity," *The Abandoned Mind* (blog), February 2, 2007, http://theabandonedmind.blogspot.com/2007_02_01_archive.html.

gle against apartheid, the Dutch Reformed Mission Church, comprised originally of mostly the "Colored" population, and then the largely black Dutch Reformed Church in Africa, understood the theological challenge and the biblical disobedience represented by the largely white Dutch Reformed Church's support of apartheid. They understood this as a question basic to the confession of faith.

In response, the Belhar Confession was drafted, and adopted by the Dutch Reformed Mission Church in 1986. That denomination merged with the largely black church to form the Uniting Reformed Church of Southern Africa.

The Belhar Confession stresses the call of the gospel to unity, justice, and reconciliation. Out of the pain of injustice and division, it crafted perhaps the most powerful call to unity ever placed in a confession of faith. My own denomination, the Reformed Church in America, studied this confession for 15 years and in 2010 adopted it as one of our own confessions — the first time in nearly 400 years that we had adopted a new confession.

In late 2011, in a historic and inspired moment, the General Synod of the largely white Dutch Reformed Church approved the Belhar Confession, sending it to their synods and congregations for action. This could open the door to an eventual union between these churches of the white, colored, and black communities — a union that would be real, visible, and a powerful sign to the world of the reconciling power of the gospel of Jesus Christ.

The first part of the Belhar Confession presents the biblical mandate for the unity of the church in as powerful a way as can be found in any confession or statement of faith. It comes as a voice speaking out of the experience of the church in the global South, and hopefully can be received by the church in the global North as a confessional and biblical affirmation of our call to belong to one another, as one body:

> We believe in one holy, universal Christian church, the communion of saints called from the entire human family.
>
> We believe
>
> that Christ's work of reconciliation is made manifest in the church as the community of believers who have been reconciled with God and with one another (Eph. 2:11-22);
>
> that unity is, therefore, both a gift and an obligation for the church of Jesus Christ; that through the working of God's Spirit it is a

binding force, yet simultaneously a reality which must be earnestly pursued and sought: one which the people of God must continually be built up to attain (Eph. 4:1-16);

that this unity must become visible so that the world may believe that separation, enmity and hatred between people and groups is sin which Christ has already conquered, and accordingly that anything which threatens this unity may have no place in the church and must be resisted (John 17:20-23);

that this unity of the people of God must be manifested and be active in a variety of ways: in that we love one another; that we experience, practice and pursue community with one another; that we are obligated to give ourselves willingly and joyfully to be of benefit and blessing to one another; that we share one faith, have one calling, are of one soul and one mind; have one God and Father, are filled with one Spirit, are baptized with one baptism, eat of one bread and drink of one cup, confess one name, are obedient to one Lord, work for one cause, and share one hope; together come to know the height and the breadth and the depth of the love of Christ; together are built up to the stature of Christ, to the new humanity; together know and bear one another's burdens, thereby fulfilling the law of Christ that we need one another and upbuild one another, admonishing and comforting one another; that we suffer with one another for the sake of righteousness; pray together; together serve God in this world; and together fight against all which may threaten or hinder this unity (Phil. 2:1-5; 1 Cor. 12:4-31; John 13:1-17; 1 Cor. 1:10-13; Eph. 4:1-6; Eph. 3:14-20; 1 Cor. 10:16-17; 1 Cor. 11:17-34; Gal. 6:2; 2 Cor. 1:3-4);

that this unity can be established only in freedom and not under constraint; that the variety of spiritual gifts, opportunities, backgrounds, convictions, as well as the various languages and cultures, are by virtue of the reconciliation in Christ, opportunities for mutual service and enrichment within the one visible people of God (Rom. 12:3-8; 1 Cor. 12:1-11; Eph. 4:7-13; Gal. 3:27-28; James 2:1-13).

This summarizes beautifully and powerfully God's heart for unity, and the resonance of this truth throughout Scripture. These words, summarizing God's Word, call us to repentance. And we are then invited into a new vision of what it means to live knowing, with all the saints, that we have all been made to drink of one Spirit, and to discover the breadth, height, length, and depth of the love of Christ, surpassing our knowledge and imagination.

Now we must ask, in light of the serious divisions in world Christianity, what possible pathways might be explored in a pilgrimage toward realizing this unity as a gift, and an obligation.

CHAPTER FIVE

Roads Well Traveled

Last year 179,919 pilgrims walked across northern Spain to the Cathedral at Santiago de Compostela, following paths begun by Christians a thousand years ago. Most of these pilgrimages take over thirty days, beginning at St. Jean Pied de Port, France, by the Spanish border. Pilgrims walk from twenty to twenty-five kilometers a day, staying at inns designed to welcome them along the way.

In medieval times, this was one of the most important pilgrimage destinations in Europe. Legend has it that the bones of the apostle James are buried in the cathedral, and in acts of devotion believers during that time would leave everything and walk for weeks on the Camino de Santiago, or the Way of St. James.

About twenty-five years ago this tradition began to be revived, with surprising results. In a continent where historic churches struggle for relevance and life, thousands of people have embarked on their own spiritual quest, following this pilgrim way, and attracting others from around the world. For many, it's like an extended retreat, and a search to find faith or to deepen one's walk with God.

I hope to make this pilgrimage. So I've been reading a guidebook, *A Pilgrim's Guide to the Camino de Santiago.* The book is subtitled *A Practical and Mystical Manual for the Modern Day Pilgrim.* It outlines the suggested route for each day, first describing the "practical path," including the terrain, pathways, possible obstacles, and the way forward. Then it describes the "mystical path," including stories about the spiritual significance of things encountered, like an ancient stone cross or a ninth-century monastery, reminding the pilgrim that this is an inward, as much as an outward, journey. The guidebook then includes personal reflections based upon experiences along each part of the way.

It struck me as I read this book that this framework could serve as a guide in today's pilgrimage of Christian unity. This will be a long journey, filled with practical complexities and challenges. We are confronted with a maze of more than 40,000 denominations in the world, along with a confusing infrastructure of various ecumenical organizations, paralleled by vast networks of evangelical churches and a growing Pentecostal movement. The Catholic Church constitutes a whole separate reality. Geographical divisions between the North and the South enforce divisive tensions around wealth and power. Vast institutional networks reinforce parochial security and identity within the divided faith families of world Christianity. It's a challenging task just to create a map of this terrain, much less to find a practical way forward. Intentional, gradual pathways need to be well planned.

But at the same time, this pilgrimage of Christian unity has to be a spiritual, mystical journey, woven into the practical steps that are taken. As we've noted before, discovering and recovering the unity of the body of Christ is not a project. At its heart, this is rooted in a deep embrace of God's truth, of Christ's love, and of the Spirit's power. The numerous Scripture passages and images beckoning us to this journey underscore that the oneness of body is a fundamental reality, and a gift. Receiving this gift then directs us to embark on a journey that is arduous, risky, and demanding.

So the practical way and the mystical way in this pilgrimage of Christian unity have to be constantly held together. Part of our failure, and some of the reason for our present predicament, is that we've kept these two ways separated. Some Christians have extolled the glory of "spiritual union" while ignoring, or even contributing to, the countless and sinful competing structures that divide the body. Others work tirelessly, in practical ways, to create mechanisms for "building" Christian unity, but neglect attention to the mystical dimensions that always need to accompany the mystery of belonging to one body.

Douglas Jacobsen's impressive, comprehensive new textbook *The World's Christians: Who They Are, Where They Are, and How They Got There* outlines the full scope of world Christianity. William Burrows, professor of missiology at New York Theological Seminary, concludes his review of the book for the *Christian Century* with this: "The theological question is whether, in the midst of the plurality that Jacobsen describes, a new kind of ecumenism will develop that is big enough to recognize a deeper unity in Christ — and then to produce the love that will make a difference."[1]

Burrows captures in that sentence the ecumenical challenge presented by the present and future realities of world Christianity. All this is made even more difficult because historic ecumenical vehicles have become far weaker just as obstacles and divisions in the global church have become far more complex and formidable.

Conciliar ecumenism and its supporting institutions find themselves at a new point of crisis. Theological dialogues over the past six decades have produced abundant fruit. But points of fundamental difference have emerged that are far more difficult to transcend theologically, and the energy for pursuing these pathways seems to be waning.

Moreover, the organizational infrastructure of conciliar ecumenism is in disrepair. The staff and budget of the World Council of Churches (WCC) have been reduced by more than half since I served on its staff, which service included the Canberra Assembly in 1991. More recently, the WCC closed its library and bookstore, and decreasing finances have resulted in serious austerity. Program expectations dramatically exceed staff capacities, and the resulting pressures often focus organizational energy around internal sustainability rather than external ecumenical vision.

The World Communion of Reformed Churches, endeavoring to live out its mandate from its organizing assembly in Grand Rapids, Michigan, in 2010, is facing severe financial constraints. It's been forced to relocate its offices outside of Geneva, a step that, in my view, it should have initiated when the merger between the World Alliance of Reformed Churches and the Reformed Ecumenical Council was first being discussed. But today its limited capacity is under serious strain.

In the United States, the National Council of Churches of Christ (USA) has faced devastating drops in income, and struggled with a $1 million shortfall in its projected budget. A transitional general secretary, hired in the middle of 2012, is trying to guide the organization toward fundamental transformation. Its staff, once over 300, occupying a large part of 475 Riverside Drive in New York, is now down to about 15. Many reports from other regional ecumenical organizations and national councils in other parts of the world tell similar stories.

---

1. William R. Burrows, review of *The World's Christians: Who They Are, Where They Are, and How They Got There*, by Douglas Jacobsen, *Christian Century*, June 27, 2012, p. 39.

But the challenges to the global ecumenical task today are not primarily institutional ones. While the struggles of various ecumenical bodies may absorb the attention of veteran ecumenists, the deepest challenges strike to the heart of how we conceive our calling to live faithfully according to the gift of unity given by God's Spirit.

As we have seen, the contours of Christianity across the globe are shifting like seismic plates, revealing new and often severe gulfs and cleavages in the global body of Christ. All this requires a fresh vision and new methodology in order to embrace the unity of the church as *"both a gift and an obligation,"* in the words of the Belhar Confession. We need to open our minds and our spiritual imaginations to the full scope of that work today. This is what is most needed at this moment — not anxiety about organizational malaise and dysfunction, but inspiration around the new and expansive horizon at hand in making manifest in the church, globally, Christ's work of reconciliation, and the unity of his body.

The Contribution of the World Council of Churches

Among the present pathways that have been trod in the search for Christian unity, the most prominent at the global level is the World Council of Churches. On a personal level, this is an organization that I treasure and deeply respect. For six years I served on its staff, originally invited to be its Director of Church and Society, and I worked on a wide range of programs in various parts of the world. Then, for another twelve years, I represented the Reformed Church in America (RCA) on the WCC Central Committee, its governing board. I've had the privilege of sharing deeply in many dimensions of its work and life.

Yet, I also bring what I hope is a fair and loving critique of the World Council of Churches. Despite my high regard for its calling, and deep respect for its leadership, I am concerned that the organization is far too consumed with its own institutional sustainability, and hindered in directing its energy and resources in creative responses to the dramatically changing landscape of world Christianity, with its deep and pervasive divisions. My sense is that it will take a transformational change in its culture and priorities to engage its core capacities around the full range of contemporary challenges of Christian unity. However, this vocation, constitutionally, remains at the heart of the WCC's calling.

Over sixty years, the list of the WCC's achievements is an impressive legacy of ecumenical progress. The sheer volume of publications, consultations, reports, advocacy work, and global gatherings is astounding. Christians from all theological backgrounds should be grateful for this work, even if they are not always in agreement with all of its results.

Yet, observers and church historians will ask, what parts of the WCC's work will have had a deep and lasting effect on the churches and in the world over the past half century? I would offer two examples: the baptism, eucharist, and ministry process from the WCC's Faith and Order work, and the efforts against apartheid from the WCC's Program to Combat Racism. While many parts in the WCC's vast array of programs and initiatives could be cited, these two, in my judgment, have made a particularly significant and long-lasting historical contribution.

The WCC's report *Baptism, Eucharist, and Ministry (BEM)* followed two decades of work, and was adopted by Faith and Order at its meeting in Lima, Peru, in 1982. Including the participation of the Catholic Church, this groundbreaking report identified those points of agreement in how churches from Orthodox, Protestant, and Catholic traditions understood the key issues of baptism, Eucharist, and ministry. And it also outlined the major and serious differences that remained. A eucharistic liturgy, informally called the "Lima Liturgy," accompanied the document, even though these major traditions could not, and today still cannot, share together in any common celebration of communion. (This was the liturgy I used for the Lord's Table when I was ordained in the Reformed Church in America [RCA] in 1984.)

The real impact of the *BEM* report came when it was sent to the WCC member churches, and others, for their reception and response. Since that time, six volumes of responses from the churches have been printed, and publication continues. The *BEM* report is in its fortieth printing. No WCC document has been more widely published, circulated, and utilized.

The *BEM* report and the dialogues that followed created a climate for churches especially in the Protestant world to engage in fresh discussions aimed at reconciling differences around these issues. For example, my own denomination, the Reformed Church in America, joined with the Presbyterian Church (USA) (PCUSA) and the United Church of Christ (UCC) in a historic agreement in 1997 with the Evangelical Lutheran Church in America, mutually recognizing one another's ministry, baptism, and communion. This officially ended divisions that had persisted between Lutheran and Reformed churches since the Reformation. Similar agreements between Lutheran and Reformed bodies have taken place elsewhere around the world.

Of even more significance, churches in the United States from the Reformed tradition (RCA, UCC, PCUSA, and the Christian Reformed Church) have been in sustained dialogue with the U.S. Catholic Church, most recently over baptism. This resulted in a remarkable agreement in 2011 recognizing mutually our baptisms across Reformed and Catholic traditions in the United States. Only a few other similar agreements exist in other places of the world.

Despite such progress, however, realism is required about the obstacles that remain. Within the member churches of the WCC, there's no mutual recognition of each other's baptisms. In planning for the WCC's Eighth Assembly in Harare in 1998, I and others proposed that those at the assembly simply witness a service of baptism of adult believers performed by a local church in Zimbabwe, as part of our gathering. But Orthodox colleagues wouldn't agree; they were worried about how that could be interpreted within their own constituencies.

Protestant observers of the ecumenical movement often do not understand that Orthodox churches cannot recognize the other members of the WCC officially as actual churches because of deep differences in ecclesiology. This became one of the early, critical questions to be resolved following the founding of the WCC in 1948. A major and formative agreement, called the Toronto Statement, was adopted in 1950 clarifying that membership in the WCC did not imply acceptance of any particular ecclesiology. This lengthy and rich explanation includes this understanding: "membership does not imply that each church must regard the other member churches as churches in the true and full sense of the word."[2] That understanding was essential for the Orthodox churches (and others) to become members of the WCC without forfeiting or compromising their self-understanding as constituting the one true undivided church.

The Toronto Statement goes on with this affirmation: "The member churches of the World Council recognize in other churches elements of

2. The Toronto Statement can be found on the WCC website at: http://www.oikou mene.org/en/resources/documents/central-committee/toronto-1950/toronto-statement .html Among various historical explanations of the Toronto Statement's history and significance, see Robert S. Bilheimer, *Breakthrough: The Emergence of the Ecumenical Tradition* (Grand Rapids: Eerdmans, 1989), pp. 47-57.

the true Church. They consider that this mutual recognition obliges them to enter into a serious conversation with each other." Such conversations have flourished in processes like baptism, Eucharist, and ministry, and progress has been made. But those core ecclesiological differences stubbornly persist.

While more nuanced, the same issue pertains to Catholic views of many other church bodies. (The Catholic Church is not a member of the WCC, but participates fully in the Faith and Order Commission.) Because of these deep ecclesiological differences, the hope of eucharistic sharing between Catholic and Protestant churches, much less with the Orthodox, remains a distant dream.

The eucharistic sharing that does take place between Catholics and Protestants today comes as a result of ecclesiastical disobedience — sometimes publicly intentional, and at other times more like "don't ask, don't tell." Those practices will only increase at the grassroots level in coming years, even as formal theological dialogues remain at an impasse. So while *BEM* has opened significant avenues for ecumenical dialogue, with some important agreements, barriers around the more fundamental question — do we actually understand one another as being part of the "church" — prevent dramatic steps forward.

Fittingly, the WCC's Faith and Order Commission has focused on the issues of ecclesiology since the time of its Fifth World Conference, held, interestingly enough, in Santiago de Compostela, Spain, in 1993. Twenty years of work with various texts produced a document, *The Church: Toward a Common Vision,* approved by the commission in 2012 and then sent to the WCC member churches for their responses.

Critics of the Faith and Order tradition of the WCC argue that theological dialogues in rarefied atmospheres between official representatives of church bodies remain detached from the struggles for justice in the world. Further, they allege, such dialogues are distant from the grassroots movements and groups inspired by the gospel that are working across denominational lines and making a real difference in the world. These voices draw on another main stream leading to the formation of the WCC, the Life and Work movement. Setting theological differences aside, this stream hoped that Christian unity could emerge from action together addressing the world's needs and injustices. The Church and Society work of the WCC, which I came to direct in 1989, stood within this tradition of the council's history and life.

By far, the vast majority of the WCC's resources, staff, and programs over the past four decades have addressed issues of global economic injustice, human rights, the role of women, global warming, racism, peacemaking, indigenous peoples, overcoming violence, and other forms of social solidarity. The scope of issues around justice, peace, care of creation, and human rights addressed by the WCC is without parallel in any global Christian organization. This breadth of commitment has existed partly because donor agencies in the past have been willing to pay for such designated programs, while funds for areas like Faith and Order have been much more difficult to find, drawing on the WCC's limited undesignated income.

Within that vast work, the Program to Combat Racism and its actions against apartheid in South Africa stand out as a testimony to the ecumenical witness of the churches for justice in the world. Internally, it was a contentious issue, serving as a source of serious controversy within the WCC and the target of sharp critique by the WCC's detractors. The underlying issue was how a church organization like the WCC could assist a movement that was unwilling to renounce violence.

But the WCC allowed those questions to be resolved within South Africa among the churches, movements, and groups on the ground. It was determined to take a prophetic stand against apartheid, and to match those words with actions, setting up a special fund to do so. The WCC's role within the deeply religious nation of South Africa was critical.

After Nelson Mandela was released from prison, and the framework for a new South Africa was being established, he traveled to Geneva to thank the WCC for its support, as well as other international organizations. His remarks in the Ecumenical Centre's Assembly Hall and a reception with WCC staff afterward were moments never to be forgotten.

Many years later while in Cape Town, I had the opportunity to visit the prison and the cell where Nelson Mandela was held for seventeen years on Robben Island, and talk with leaders from the Reformed churches in South Africa — white and black. The pathways toward reconciliation and unity within that society through a remarkably nonviolent transition, though still deeply challenging, have been undergirded by the strength of Christian witness. The WCC, through its prophetic actions years earlier, placed itself on the right side of history in ways that helped make a decisive difference.

But what of the World Council of Churches' present, and its future?

As the WCC approaches its Tenth Assembly in Busan, Korea, in 2013, it finds itself at a crossroads. First, the WCC will have to decide how to cope with a future of diminishing financial resources, and learn to succeed in its long struggle of determining which programs it should stop doing. That's essential if it is to focus its available capacity and find ways to make unique and needed contributions in the future pilgrimage toward Christian unity. Those who do the work of organizational transformation quickly learn that "the good can be the enemy of the best." That is abundantly true for the programmatic life of the World Council of Churches.

Second, the WCC has to demonstrate that it is able to function as a vibrant fellowship of its member churches, as they engage each other and act together, rather than behave as a bureaucratic program agency doing things on behalf of the churches. This was at the heart of the WCC's Common Understanding and Vision, a serious process of self-reflection resulting in a major statement adopted in 1996. Years later, however, the question remains as to whether this has fundamentally changed how the WCC lives and acts. A frequent worry of those close to the WCC is that its advocacy work on a wide range of social and economic issues, however admirable, makes it seem simply like another international nongovernmental organization (NGO). Its Common Understanding and Vision process intended to focus its unique identity on the relationships between its member churches, empowering them in their mutual witness and service.

Third, and perhaps most important, is whether the WCC can commit itself wholeheartedly to engage the vast number of denominations that live completely outside the ecumenical movement, and to serve as a bridge between the major divisions in world Christianity today. Two numbers summarize the predicament — and the potential opportunity — of the WCC: 349 — the number of member churches belonging today to the WCC; 43,800 — the number of Christian denominations estimated now to exist in the world.

When the WCC was founded in 1948, it included 147 member churches. Adding members has been a slow process, with about 200 churches being added in sixty-five years. Meanwhile, as we have seen, the sheer number of denominations in the world has grown astronomically. During the decades when the WCC was doing its careful, patient work, the pilgrimage of world Christianity had transformed the global church in revolutionary ways. The clear challenge facing the WCC is that it has lived in relative isolation from streams and movements that are shaping the future of Christianity in the world.

The fast-growing Pentecostal churches, energetic evangelical churches throughout the global South, congregations of the African Instituted Churches, and other highly contextualized forms of emerging Christianity function in ecclesiological worlds almost completely separate from traditional ecumenical structures. When the WCC adds up the numbers of all those who belong to its member churches, they use the figure of 560 million, or about one-quarter of the world's Christian community. This is bolstered by the large membership of Orthodox churches belonging to the WCC.

But most observers studying the trends shaping the pilgrimage of world Christianity agree that the dynamism and growth driving the future of the church, especially in the global South, are coming from those parts of the Christian family that have little or no connection to the WCC or other ecumenical bodies. As stated previously, the gulf between these newly emerging churches and those long-established, historic churches constitutes the most serious challenge to nurturing unity within world Christianity.

The WCC's Tenth Assembly in Korea in 2013 offers an opportunity for new ways forward that could address these challenges. But this would require a fundamental shift, and a commitment to deep change, revitalizing the culture and style of the WCC as well as the nature of its work. The bureaucratic momentum, pressures of specific constituencies, and institutional baggage characterizing the WCC's organizational life are substantial, as with any organization of its history and size. Changing these would be a difficult task, but not unlike that undertaken by other church organizations in today's world seeking deep transformation in their mission and work.

Moving in such directions also would require deep reflection and careful discernment. Recall the framework proposed for the church's journey toward unity: the practical steps, the mystical/spiritual dimension, and the time for reflection. Following the Busan Assembly, I would hope that the WCC would claim a "Jubilee Year," entering into a sabbatical time, devoted to probing discernment about its life and future. The results of the assembly would receive sustained reflection. Instead of immediately restarting all the WCC's programs and activities, staff and the newly elected governing body members would ask the most important questions about the WCC's future during this Jubilee

Year, and provide an open space in worship, prayer, dialogue, and discernment for the work of God's Spirit as answers are sought.

There's power in such a pause from doing business as usual, and effective organizational transformation typically requires the creation of such a space. Certainly this draws on the wisdom of the jubilee and sabbatical biblical traditions. Further, the necessary time between a WCC assembly and the initial meeting of its newly elected Central Committee can lend itself to such a jubilee period for both staff and governing board members.

Then, the WCC could make a primary commitment of outreach to the vast number of denominations and groups that are outside of the ecumenical world. In practical terms, this would require an intentional commitment of resources and staff time from its present annual budget, which totals about $30 million. As an example, for instance, consider the impact if fifty WCC staff members each visited 10 different denominations outside of the ecumenical world in the course of a year. In six years, 3,000 such churches would have a promising point of contact with the worldwide fellowship of churches. The changes that could come would be creative and richly fruitful.

Other structural changes might result. For instance, the present process for a new denomination to become a member church of the WCC is long, arduous, and bureaucratic. What if another means of affiliation were established that could draw churches into an initial form of fellowship? Changes of this sort would be essential if the WCC hopes to serve as a place that welcomes the growing diversity of the world's Christian community.

The WCC has opened some initial pathways in this direction. At its Harare Assembly in 1998 a Joint Consultative Group between the WCC and Pentecostals was established. It has built a solid foundation of dialogue and interchange. Further, through initiatives begun at the Global Christian Forum meeting in Limuru, Kenya, in 2007, the WCC's general secretary, Olav Fykse Tveit, addressed the Pentecostal World Conference in Stockholm, in 2010. Such exchanges are building trust and opening up doors.

Moreover, some Pentecostal denominations have expressed interest in becoming members of the WCC, joining half a dozen or so who already belong, such as the Pentecostal Church of Chile and the Evangelical Pentecostal Mission of Angola. This is an encouraging sign. Yet, it raises other difficulties. In the last decade, a serious process has been devoted to establishing clarity and proper recognition for the role of the Orthodox churches in the WCC. Years of work by a Special Commission on Relations with the Orthodox, established at the Harare Assembly in 1998, have helped significantly to deepen the trust of Orthodox within the WCC and change procedures in ways that secure their voice and influence in the council.

Many Orthodox, however, have concerns about the prospects of expanding Pentecostal membership. Their potential numbers, theoretically, could overwhelm the Orthodox presence in the WCC. Moreover, the ecclesiological gulf between Pentecostals and Orthodox is huge. Based on difficult experiences within their national settings, many Orthodox regard Pentecostals as proliferating sectarian movements aimed at proselytizing members from their churches.

Any widespread and serious incorporation of numerous Pentecostal churches in the WCC — however distant a possibility that may seem today — would require serious changes in the WCC's culture and style, as well as a fresh reflection on the expanded ecclesiological diversity this would bring. In many ways, however, this would parallel the theological work that was necessary before the Orthodox became members of the WCC. Significant Pentecostal participation in the WCC would require changes in the same fashion that has been necessary for Orthodox participation in the council. Perhaps even a new understanding similar to the Toronto Statement would be needed. But that's precisely the agenda the WCC should be willing to embrace to open a horizon for expanded Pentecostal membership.

Any discussions about expanding participation to Pentecostals, evangelicals, and other nonmember churches raise the question about what would happen to the historic commitments of the WCC to its witness for justice and peace, and its widespread advocacy work. First, it's clear that these commitments are deeply imbedded in the DNA of the World Council of Churches. From the beginning, those pioneers who established the WCC understood that the church's unity was for the world. That central commitment, seen as intrinsic to the witness of Christian faith, will not be altered by any WCC governing body.

Further, with the shift of the vast majority of evangelical and Pentecostal churches to the global South, their own agenda around questions of social justice has begun to reflect their context. That is apparent in the issues being addressed by the World Evangelical Alliance. Further, many indigenous Pentecostal churches, especially when not linked to parent bodies in the global North, take root particularly among the poor and marginalized in their societies. While a diversity of views exists, including the "prosperity gospel," it's clear from several initiatives that common ground can be found between those in the ecumenical community and evangelicals and Pentecostals — especially those from the global South who are open to wider fellowship — around critical matters of justice, peace, and advocacy.

But with or without expanded membership in the WCC, it will be essential for the body to consider how its advocacy work can be selected, focused, and prioritized in coming years. Thankfully, church-related groups addressing issues of justice, peace, creation, and human solidarity on a global level now abound. The WCC's challenge following the Busan Assembly will be to discern where, over a period of six or seven years, the WCC might be able to make a genuine and unique contribution on a very narrow number of issues, as it did on apartheid. Its prophetic role should find such a sharp and well-defined profile, rather than being overextended by a smorgasbord of tempting options.

Finally, the WCC should make a commitment to move its headquarters out of Geneva, Switzerland, to a location in the global South. This would send a dramatic message that this sixty-year-old institution recognizes the dramatic changes in world Christianity and is committed to changing itself in response. Financially, the continued presence of the WCC in the world's fifth most expensive city becomes increasingly hard to justify as proper stewardship.

Faced with severe financial shortfalls, the WCC presently is realizing that its building, and even more, its land, in a beautiful location on the outskirts of Geneva, is its most valuable asset. It plans to capitalize on this asset, and develop its property into an income-producing resource. And certainly, one can make a strong argument for remaining in Geneva's milieu of other international organizations. Yet, at some point, the headquarters of an organization committed to seeking the unity of the church should place itself in the settings that are driving the future of world Christianity.

All these steps would face serious resistance from many quarters. But in my judgment, this focuses the choices that are before the WCC as it approaches the Busan Assembly. It would take the assembly to mandate these kinds of general directions to its newly elected Central Committee.

The body of Christ through the world is undergoing massive shifts and changes, with new divisions that mock the promise of the unity given by God. My hope is that the WCC can fundamentally transform itself in order to play a key role in today's pilgrimage of Christian unity. Certainly it's tempting to remain in its familiar world, largely isolated from the growing parts of the Christian world that can offer such mutual enrichment, so needed in the discovery of becoming one, as Jesus prayed. But the WCC has the opportunity to imagine in fresh and creative ways how to express its core constitutional vocation, as follows: "The primary purpose of the fellowship of churches in the World Council of Churches is to call one another to visible unity in one faith and in one eucharistic fellowship, expressed in worship and common life in Christ, through witness and service to the world, and to advance towards that unity in order that the world may believe."[3]

3. Constitution and Rules of the World Council of Churches, Section III, Purposes and Functions, paragraph 2.

CHAPTER SIX

New Pathways

In 1988, forest fires swept through Yellowstone Park. As individual fires combined with accelerating force, these fires became the most severe in the known history of this spectacular region. They burned out of control for weeks and even months, and nine thousand firefighters fought to contain the blaze. On September 8, for the first time in its history, Yellowstone Park was closed to visitors.

The fires did not subside until late in the fall, when falling temperatures combined with rain and snow to assist the massive efforts of helicopters, planes, and firefighters. By that time, 36 percent of Yellowstone Park experienced the devastating effects of these fires. Many worried that the scarred landscape would ruin Yellowstone, the nation's first national park, and end its widespread attraction to visitors from the United States and around the world.

My family and I love Yellowstone Park, and began visiting there before the 1988 fires, when we lived in Montana. Returning after the 1988 fires, we were at first shocked by scenes of apparent devastation. Charred tree trunks littered the mountainsides of the Madison Valley and the Firehole River Canyon. Areas on the spectacular Dunraven Pass were like a wasteland. Carnage had swept right up to the Old Faithful Inn. Yellowstone Park felt like a different place, carrying the wounds of this destructive chapter.

Yet, even on that visit we saw signs of surprising hope. Many areas beneath charred ruins were like a lush green carpet. We learned that the depth of charred soil was only about one-half inch, so roots of grasses and plants remained. Now exposed to sunlight, they rapidly sprang to life. Then, wildflowers began to burst forth in abundance, more plentiful than before.

Even more surprising, on subsequent visits we saw shoots of new pine trees beginning to grow, in the tens of thousands. Park rangers explained that the lodgepole pine trees, which dominated in several areas of the park, and often burned ferociously, carried an amazing process of regeneration. Most pine cones from the lodgepole pine do not release their seeds unless they are subjected to the high temperatures of fire. Thus, areas of intense fire now were witnessing widespread growth of new lodgepole pine.

Aspen trees began appearing miles from the few previous groves of aspen. It wasn't commonly thought that aspen could regenerate from such seed dispersal rather than from their roots, but the fires brought new and unexpected changes to the landscape of the park. Such changes have proved very beneficial to wildlife, producing new habitats and sources of food.

Today, Yellowstone Park preaches sermons filled with the metaphors of death and surprising rebirth. It provides a living testimony from the creation of the power of regeneration that functions like intrinsic natural grace. Walking through emerging new and lush growth surrounding the remains of charred trees, one can't help but be moved by surprising possibilities of renewal.

These experiences in Yellowstone prompt reflection on the dynamics of organizational transformation and the emergence of new movements. This is especially true when considering the complex ecumenical landscape surrounding world Christianity. Of course, all metaphors have limitations. Certainly, I don't want to suggest that the historic, existing ecumenical structures have suffered widespread devastation. Yet, the weaknesses of these structures in the face of the accelerating change that is sweeping across the contours of world Christianity are evident.

But what is most striking are the surprising signs of ongoing resilience in the quest to transcend divisions and nurture expressions of our common belonging to one body. Many of these are grassroots efforts, often springing up spontaneously, and drawing together Christians from separated backgrounds. In countless settings, such initiatives occur around efforts to build houses for the disadvantaged, to respond to destructive natural tragedies, to make a witness for peace in places of violence, to coordinate work to overcome poverty, to address world hunger, and similar examples. These efforts continue to sprout up, grow, and spread.

Likewise, movements of prayer and worship, determined to reach across confessional barriers, continue to find life. Most visible is the Week of Prayer for Christian Unity. Begun in 1908 through the influence of Father Paul Wattson, a Franciscan Friar of the Atonement, this observance became jointly sponsored by the WCC's Faith and Order Commission and the Vatican's Pontifical Council for Promoting Christian Unity in 1968. The Graymoor Ecumenical and Interreligious Institute, a ministry of the Franciscan Friars of the Atonement, provides resources and support for the observance of this Week of Prayer, which takes place in January in the Northern Hemisphere and during Pentecost in the global South.

United in Christ is an initiative from Pentecostals and charismatics seeking to build unity among Catholics and Pentecostals through a shared experience of the Holy Spirit. Its third gathering was held in Toronto in December 2012. The Community of Saint'Egidio is a lay movement in the Catholic tradition working for peace and solidarity with the poor, with a deep commitment to ecumenism. Begun in 1968, it has 50,000 members in seventy countries. Examples like this abound, and are flourishing.

Clearly, while wounds and scars mar the ecumenical landscape, and the structures of "old growth" seem vulnerable as they struggle to sustain themselves, the roots of new life nurturing the gift of unity are just beneath the surface, and widespread. Surprising new growth is breaking forth, often intermingled with the old in ways that bring regeneration to the whole ecumenical ecosystem.

The Emergence of the Global Christian Forum

On the global level, the most promising new initiative to emerge addressing the major divisions in world Christianity is the Global Christian Forum. Arising out of the World Council of Churches at its Eighth Assembly in Harare in 1998, and then becoming autonomous, the forum has become a fresh and credible movement that offers a real hope of transcending these divisions.

Uniquely, this "new growth" in ecumenism has been successfully engaging leaders of all the major Christian traditions — Catholic, Pentecostal, evangelical, Orthodox, and historic Protestant — in a new place of global fellowship. Global gatherings in Limuru, Kenya, in 2007 and in Manado, Indonesia, in 2011 broke new ground in ecumenical history. So it's important to reflect on both the practical and the mystical dimensions of this fresh pathway in the pilgrimage of Christian unity.

The World Council of Churches played a primary role in giving birth to the Global Christian Forum. Dr. Konrad Raiser, general secretary from 1993 to 2003, outlined the challenge facing the WCC, stating that world Christianity could be divided into four main families — Catholic, historic Protestant, evangelical/Pentecostal, and Orthodox. The WCC's membership comprised for the most part only two of those families — historic Protestant and Orthodox. A new "ecumenical space" had to be found to draw together leaders from the full breadth of world Christianity, establishing a place of ongoing relationship, fellowship, and interchange.

With Dr. Raiser's support, this search for a "forum" or initiative reaching out to the wider Christian world was articulated at the Eighth Assembly of the WCC in 1998. Following that event, tentative, exploratory meetings were held first at Bossey, Switzerland, and then two meetings at Fuller Theological Seminary in Pasadena, California, in 2000 and 2002. The purpose was to test this idea, especially with Pentecostal, evangelical, and Catholic leaders. If they weren't interested, there would have been no point in pursuing this idea further.

But the leaders invited to these early conversations responded positively. They sensed the need for a place of fellowship drawing together Christians normally isolated from one another, living in separate institutional and ecclesiological worlds. This positive response came with the advice that this model first be proposed and tested in various regions around the world. A draft purpose statement was also developed in 2002 that included this description of the Global Christian Forum's intent: "To create an open space wherein representatives from a broad range of Christian churches and interchurch organizations, which confess the triune God and Jesus Christ as perfect in His divinity and humanity, can gather together to foster mutual respect, to explore and to address common challenges."

It also became clear from the start that such an initiative would have to function independently from the WCC. A long history of suspicion and mistrust toward the WCC, particularly from evangelical and Pentecostal groups, could not be easily overcome. If this new venture functioned simply as another program controlled by the WCC, it would unfortunately drive away many of those whose presence was most important to its success.

What followed was an inspiring demonstration of ecumenical humility and hospitality on the part of the WCC. Although being the prime mover in launching this initiative, the WCC also liberated it. A group originally called the "Continuation Committee," with representatives from various church and organizational bodies that were engaged in the process, was given the authority to govern, guide, and direct this newly emerging idea.

At the same time, the World Council of Churches provided an infrastructure of administrative support. Further, a veteran WCC staff member, Hubert van Beek, whose commitment was focused on relating to those groups outside of the WCC's membership, was assigned to provide staff support. When he later retired from the WCC, van Beek provided the endless energy, persistent effort, seasoned wisdom, and undaunted determination to make the Global Christian Forum a reality.

Sitting in front of his computer screen in his apartment in Versoix, Switzerland, overlooking Lake Geneva, van Beek spent thousands of hours in those first years building the relational infrastructure of the Global Christian Forum. He was in touch with Orthodox bishops in Romania, Pentecostal leaders from Ghana, evangelical pastors in India, officials at the Vatican, Protestant leaders in the United States — all in all, with the diverse scope of leadership in world Christianity. His goal was to bring them together, which had never happened before. And the database he developed became probably the most diverse and comprehensive list of those in various leadership positions in their churches and Christian organizations that exists anywhere in the world.

With the guidance of the Continuation Committee, a series of regional consultations in Asia, Africa, Europe, and Latin America were held that further tested the idea of the Global Christian Forum. I remember well the African consultation, held in Lusaka, Zambia, in 2005. About seventy church leaders from all parts of Africa, and all parts of Christ's body, gathered together. They represented denominations and Christian organizations that included Baptist, Anglican, Pentecostal, Reformed, Roman Catholic, Orthodox, Seventh-Day Adventist, evangelical, and Lutheran churches, as well as the All Africa Christian Council, the Association of Evangelicals in Africa, the International Fellowship of Evangelical Students, the World Student Christian Federation, World Vision, the United Bible Societies, the African

Theological Fellowship, various national councils of churches, and the African Instituted Churches.

Many had never met one another before, and could not recall a comparable gathering ever taking place in Africa. As in other meetings, much of the first day and a half was spent inviting the participants to share their personal stories of faith.

The gathering then turned to the realities facing the church in Africa today. Most gripping was the devastating challenge posed to much of Africa by the HIV/AIDS crisis. The gathering spent a significant amount of time focusing on both the theological and the practical challenges confronting the churches from this crisis.

Brigalia Bam, the veteran ecumenist then in South Africa, and Kwabena Asamoah-Gyadu, a noted evangelical theologian from Ghana, each addressed the group on "Our Journey with Christ in Africa." The group identified several other areas of social and political concern that were widely shared, including combating corruption and other measures to strengthen "good governance." The natural way in which this gathering embraced the necessity of the church to be strongly involved in social action, while also giving clear attention to personal evangelism and spiritual renewal, seemed remarkable. There was no serious controversy over those issues, despite the wide diversity of churches and organizations present, and despite the fact that many had never met with one another before.

Rev. Ekow Badu Wood, of the Ghana Pentecostal Council, described this gathering of the Global Christian Forum: "This has been a beautiful opportunity for churches that have been marginalized to be given the opportunity to speak." His words bear reflection, for, like others, he shared the clear sense of previously being marginalized from the ecumenical community.

Bishop Silas Yego, head of the African Inland Church, explained that in the past his church never would have associated with the WCC or other ecumenical bodies. But at the end of the gathering, he told the group that he had never been in a meeting like this, and, filled with gratitude, was determined to build similar bridges in his own context.

Rev. Daniel Bitros, a pastor in the Church of Christ in Nigeria and former general secretary of the Evangelical Fellowship of Africa, put it this way: "A stone has been moved from off the top of the hill, and now it is rolling. There is no other ecumenical body that could have brought us together in this way. Now we have to make this concrete."

An Asian regional meeting to explore the Global Christian Forum, also in 2005, produced a positive response as well. It was jointly sponsored by the Christian Conference of Asia, the Federation of Asian Bishops' Conferences (Catholic), and the Evangelical Fellowship of Asia. Richard Howell, a participant who was general secretary of the Evangelical Fellowship of India, said this: "The Global Christian Forum is the best thing that could have happened to the Christian Church in Asia. It created an open space where people could come together for the first time to share their stories and faith journey. The Church in Asia is growing, and growth brings challenges. The Global Christian Forum gave an opportunity for those from different traditions to listen. We discovered one another. And we discovered Christ at work within our different traditions."

The next year a European gathering, held in Warburg, Germany, created a safe space for a small group of Pentecostals, evangelicals, Orthodox, Protestants, Catholics, and migrant church representatives to come together with fruitful results. A Latin American meeting in Santiago de Chile followed, including significant Roman Catholic participation. By that time the vision of the Global Christian Forum had been tested in all the major regions of the world, and had met with strong and often enthusiastic affirmation.

Three words can best describe the space and style that have emerged in the process of the Global Christian Forum: testimonial, relational, and missional. From its first exploratory meetings in Bossey and Fuller Seminary, those who gathered decided to begin by sharing with each other the stories of their journeys of faith in Christ. This simple exercise established a starting point of trust rather than division. More by discovery than by design, this became a key part of the methodology of the Global Christian Forum.

When a woman Anglican bishop from Canada shares her vision from Christ, who called her into ministry as a teenager, with a Pentecostal leader from Ghana, who was called out of business into the church, and then an Orthodox bishop from Syria shares his dramatic spiritual journey, a profound sense of belonging to one another, transcending entrenched divisions and stereotypes, is created. These become mystical moments crystallizing the truth of sharing one faith, one Lord, and one baptism. Every gathering of the Global Christian Forum begins in this way, and sometimes this takes a whole day. But this establishes a foundation of relational and spiritual trust for what follows.

The regional consultations laid the groundwork for the first world gathering of the Global Christian Forum, held in Limuru, Kenya, in 2007. About 240 Christian leaders gathered together; half were Pentecostal and evangelical. Observers called this a "watershed in modern Christian history." What happened there touched a nerve among so many participants who had been yearning for a fuller expression of Christian *koinonia* today. The final message from the Limuru gathering was met with a spontaneous doxology from the participants. The shared feeling was that something new was being born in their midst, and that this was a work of God's Spirit.

Headlines of news stories written about this gathering convey its historic importance:

- "'Historic' World Christian Forum Issues Call for Dialogue"
- "Evangelicals and Pentecostals Look to New Forms of Unity"
- "Death and Rebirth Are Needed If the Visible Unity of the Church Is to Be Achieved, Pentecostal Scholar Says"
- "Vatican Official Says World Forum for Christianity Is Vital"
- "Pentecostal Hails World Christian Forum"
- "Let's Take Risks, Kobia (WCC General Secretary) Tells Global Christian Forum"
- "Most Diverse Christian Gathering Ever to Discuss Unity and Common Witness"[1]

The Limuru gathering also called for a thorough evaluation of the Global Christian Forum's progress and process up to that time, including the results of the Limuru meeting. The Continuation Committee embraced that task energetically. Two major evaluations were conducted, one by the Oxford Mission Study Centre in England and the other by the Center IIMO at Utrecht University in the Netherlands. A third evaluation studied the perspectives of the Latin American participants.

The evaluations were thorough and detailed; the first two reports each totaled about eighty pages, and involved questioning those who

---

1. A full account of the Limuru, Kenya, meeting of the Global Christian Forum is found in Huibert van Beek, ed., *Revisioning Christian Unity: Journeying with Jesus Christ, the Reconciler, at the Global Christian Forum, Limuru, November 2007* (Oxford: Regnum International, 2009).

participated in the Limuru gathering as well as other church leaders. The overall conclusions underscored how the Global Christian Forum had succeeded in achieving its initial purpose. In the words of the Oxford Mission Study Centre Report: "The Global Christian Forum has been a very remarkable and worthwhile initiative which has sought to introduce a new sort of ecumenism. It has sought to bring together leaders of all the main Christian traditions, from the South and the North, so that they might meet together, have fellowship together, learn more about each other, and thus build up trust and relationships in a non-threatening environment. In this aim the GCF has succeeded. This in itself is a remarkable achievement and well worth pursuing further."[2]

Other conclusions in the evaluations underscored the need for further communication about the Global Christian Forum's vision and accomplishments, and also pointed with some concern to the extremely minimal infrastructure supporting this far-ranging work. A consultation representing all the churches and organizations supporting the Global Christian Forum took place in New Delhi in 2008 to review the evaluations and make plans for the next three years. This included an extensive visit of Global Christian Forum representatives to the Middle East and further meetings in Europe, Asia, Africa, and Latin America.

Those steps prepared the way for the second global meeting of the Global Christian Forum in Manado, Indonesia, in October 2011. Nearly 300 gathered from sixty-five countries and explored the theme "Life Together in Jesus Christ, Empowered by the Holy Spirit." Half were from Pentecostal and evangelical backgrounds, with the others from Orthodox, historic Protestant, and Catholic churches, as well as ecumenical organizations. As participants gathered from all corners of the globe on the first evening, I recall what a woman named Emily Obwaka, who worked with the Evangelical Alliance in Africa, said to me as we rode together on a bus: "This must be pleasing to God's heart."

The Manado global gathering attempted to move the Global Christian Forum's process forward. Beginning as always with time in small groups to share the stories of personal spiritual journeys, the program then moved to share accounts of "what the Spirit is saying to the churches" from specific places. This included the inspiring story of the resurrection of the church in Albania, an account of developments in

2. Van Beek, *Revisioning Christian Unity,* p. 198. The full text of all three evaluation reports is included in this book.

the churches in China, the reconciliation between Lutherans and Mennonites over unconfessed sins from centuries past, the witness of the Taizé community, and the struggle of the churches in the Middle East.

Other presentations included the changes in world Christianity and the understanding of the Holy Spirit from an Orthodox perspective as well as from an African Pentecostal point of view. As those who gathered worked to discern future directions, it began to be clear that the discovery of trust across stereotypes and divisions was creating a foundation from which to begin addressing challenges involving disagreement and tension.

At the closing worship service, five participants from different regions and traditions who were experiencing the Global Christian Forum for the first time shared in the sermon. They each spoke of the joy, and often the surprise, in what they discovered — some of them interacting with those from Christian traditions they barely knew even existed. The unity of heart and Spirit they experienced had a profound effect. The overall sense of most all the participants was one of joy and affirmation.

The concluding paragraph of the message that emerged from Manado says this: "The space created by the Global Christian Forum is God's gift. In a fragmented world and church, this unique expression of unity, embracing the breadth of world Christianity, is a source of inspiration and hope. We believe it is a helpful model for building authentic Christian relationships in every place. We know that God's Spirit draws the body of Christ into unity for the sake of God's mission in the world. So we commit ourselves to nurture the Global Christian Forum, as the Spirit leads, as a witness to God's saving and transforming love."

Many who were there spoke of carrying forth the Global Christian Forum's vision to relationships between churches in their home countries. Indeed, that is one of the main areas of emphasis in its future work. Through follow-up consultations in key regions and countries, as well as beginning to address global challenges of common concern, this work will build on the strength and direction of the gathering in Manado, Indonesia.

The Pentecostal World Fellowship, the World Council of Churches, the World Evangelical Alliance, and the Pontifical Council for Promoting Christian Unity at the Vatican are the four key organizations now jointly supporting the Global Christian Forum. Nearly all the Christian world communions — the Lutheran World Federation, the

Mennonite World Conference, the World Communion of Reformed Churches, the Organization of African Instituted Churches, and several others — also offer support in tangible ways.

Nevertheless, the Global Christian Forum is a very modest and fragile initiative. It has only one staff person, and an annual budget of about $200,000 (US). In the face of the overwhelming complexity and diversity of world Christianity, it seems like a mustard seed. But one wonders if it could grow and flourish, eventually providing a place to draw together the myriad expressions of Christianity through experiencing their belonging through Christ to one another and recognizing their common roots.

So the soil is fertile, supporting fresh efforts that spring up as unexpected new growth, giving hope for the future. Yet, in the pilgrimage of Christian unity within the changing landscape of world Christianity, the old and the new must learn that they need each other, and walk together. Specifically, the historic work and achievements of the World Council of Churches have an essential role to play as we journey to the future. The depth of theological discourse on crucial areas of disagreement must be carried forward. Likewise, the mobilization of the global church's voice and action on questions essential to a just and sustainable future must continually be empowered.

In 1974, Willem Visser 't Hooft wrote a short, provocative book, *Has the Ecumenical Movement a Future?* Almost four decades later, his words still hold wisdom: "Merely to say no and to turn our backs on the existing ecumenical movement would be a desperate remedy and an act of sheer ingratitude. We have no right to throw away all that has been given to us in the movement in the past forty years. What we are free to do is renew it, purify it and adapt it to present tasks."[3]

But now, the historic commitments of the WCC and other regional and national councils of churches must be accompanied by radical new initiatives to bridge the sharp divides that sever parts of the body from one another. That's what makes the particular vocation of the Global Christian Forum, and similar expressions at national and regional levels, so essential. We have no hope of forging an effective and believable Christian witness in today's and tomorrow's world without an uncompromised and courageous commitment to create the space that draws

3. Willem Visser 't Hooft, *Has the Ecumenical Movement a Future?* (Atlanta: John Knox, 1974), p. 53.

the Orthodox, Catholic, historic Protestant, and Pentecostal/evangeli-
cal communities into sustained and cooperative fellowship.

In 1949, Oliver Tomkins, who became secretary of Faith and Order
in the WCC, wrote this: "God has given his people in our days a new insight into what He wants them to do; one fruit of it is the official, organized ecumenical movement, with the World Council as its chief expression; but the essence of it, ecumenicity, is something which happens in
the souls of Christians. It is a new understanding of the Body of Christ . . .
a deep spiritual traffic, a bond of spirit so strong that it will not allow to
fly apart those who are under great pressure to become separated."[4]

That essence is what must be recovered and nurtured, in both old
and new pathways, on the pilgrimage of Christian unity.

4. Oliver Tomkins, *The Wholeness of the Church* (London: SCM, 1949), pp. 13-15,
quoted in Robert S. Bilheimer, *Breakthrough: The Emergence of the Ecumenical Tradition*
(Grand Rapids: Eerdmans, 1989), p. 217.

CHAPTER SEVEN

Signposts along the Way

Pilgrimages need signposts. As world Christianity recenters itself in the global South and East, the search to discover our belonging to one another, as one body, is a pilgrimage of Christian unity. As we go forward, attentive to both the practical steps and the mystical qualities of this pilgrimage, we can't be at all sure about knowing where our paths may lead. Much will be revealed only as we continue to step forward, with courage and faithfulness. But we can look for some signposts — some qualities and characteristics that should accompany our progress and encourage us to take the next steps. Here are five that might help show us the way.

1. Space for New Relationships

The rapidly changing realities of world Christianity are in contrast to traditional ecumenical efforts that, despite their accomplishments, function more like closed systems. In large measure, experienced people from a predictable set of churches and organizations cycle through their meetings and encounters. This underscores the urgent need for new networks of relationships to be built. These networks need to be intentionally created in ways that cross the divisions of geography, theology, institutions, and generations. Hopefully, such networks could multiply in diverse, growing ways.

Any historian of the ecumenical movement will underscore how much of the early efforts by pioneers like Willem Visser 't Hooft and John R. Mott were spent building relationships of trust within divergent parts of the Christian world. Mott traveled 2 million miles, for instance, in an era before jet airplanes, as he built the World Student Christian Association.[1] Visser 't Hooft's patient outreach to global church leaders is legendary. It remains the fact that so much of the foundation of historic ecumenical breakthroughs has depended upon building personal relationships of trust that reach over and beyond persistent divisions.

Today we need renewed, focused efforts of similar passion and commitment, connecting literally to thousands of Christian leaders, and especially to younger emerging leaders, in all parts of the world. So many of those needed to create the future expressions of Christian unity have not been invited to join this pilgrimage. Relationships to do so simply don't exist, and have to be established. Creating the new spaces to do this — both geographical and virtual — is a fundamental necessity.

Creativity is required. Why not invite 100 key young emerging leaders from evangelical, Pentecostal, Orthodox, historic Protestant, and Catholic backgrounds around the world to take a pilgrimage together to Santiago de Compostela? Or why not be more expansive in our imagination? In 1985 Pope John Paul II instituted the World Youth Day. Held about every two or three years, this event has drawn hundreds of thousands of largely Catholic young people who make pilgrimages from around the world to this celebration. In 1995, the World Youth Day drew an estimated 5 million young people to its celebration in Luneta Park, Manila, the Philippines. Rio de Janeiro is the site for the 2013 observance, and arrangements are coordinated through the Catholic Pilgrim Office.

But what would happen if a commitment was made to hold a gathering of young people not confined to just one part of the global Christian family? What would happen if the Vatican, the World Council of Churches, the World Evangelical Alliance, the Pentecostal World Fellowship, and the Ecumenical Patriarchate committed themselves to jointly sponsor a world gathering of Christian youth, drawing hundreds of thousands? Imagine what that could do in creating a massive foundational infrastructure of relationships that would dramatically influence the pilgrimage of world Christianity.

On a more modest level, ecumenical meetings, consultations, and assemblies commonly establish quotas for the number of women,

1. Mark Galli, "Mission and Ecumenism: John R. Mott," ChristianHistory.net, January 1, 2000; http://www.christianitytoday.com/ch/2000/issue65/9.36.html.

youth, and other underrepresented groups when they gather. These are proactive measures designed to give voice to those who otherwise would be marginalized from participation. Often they are.a source of contentious debate at such meetings. But what would happen if every ecumenical meeting made a commitment that at least one-third of those who gathered were people who had never been involved in such meetings? What if there was always a commitment to bring into the room, and around the table, those from different Christian traditions, backgrounds, and circumstances who had not been included in ecumenical circles?

We find ourselves at a point in the pilgrimage of Christian unity where creating space for new relationships that cross the major dividing barriers is more important than the normal programs and activities that capture our energy as well as the attention of donors. A new mindset is required that prioritizes this need, and reflects the pioneering spirit of those who painstakingly trod the early paths of Christian unity.

2. Welcoming One Another's Narratives

The fresh pathways of this pilgrimage won't begin with a fixation on points of theological difference, but with a fascination about the development of one another's spiritual journey. More attention will be placed on faith formation than on doctrinal formulation.

This isn't to ignore the importance of theological dialogue and the search for consensus over dividing issues. But we need a new way to help us go both beneath and beyond present points of theological impasse. More than this, it's essential that the stories of how we come to faith, and grow in faith, accompany our explanations of what we theologically believe.

Still further, there's a wide gulf between the engagement of theologians in important bilateral and multilateral dialogues, and the participation of pastors, church leaders, young people, and others in the life and outreach of the churches. Additionally, many of the new partners in the future pilgrimage of Christian unity come with very different agendas, and have not been engaged in the traditional agenda of theological debate in ecumenical circles.

For all these reasons, new "on-ramps" leading people into the pilgrimage of Christian unity are required. These will be created by welcoming, reflecting on, and learning from the narratives of each other's spiritual journeys.

This is not just a theory, or an idea. It's rooted and tested in experience, especially through the Global Christian Forum, but elsewhere as well. When we gather with those coming from very different traditions of the Christian faith, but take the time to offer the respect to listen deeply to the stories of their spiritual journeys, we enter into "holy ground." I've seen this, and participated in this process repeatedly, in gatherings with younger people, in retreats with those charged to lead denominations, in gatherings of African church leaders, in ecumenical circles from the widest geographical and theological diversity, and in those memorable global meetings in Limuru, Kenya, and Manado, Indonesia. This is one way we will discover the mystical path of our pilgrimage to sustain us in the face of hard practical challenges.

3. Singing the Lord's Song

When the children of Israel made their pilgrimage up to Jerusalem, they sang together the Psalms of Ascent. Those pathways toward unity were sustained by worship, prayer, and shared spiritual practices. Ours today must be as well.

One of the contemporary ecumenical ironies is that the way many congregations — in North America and in Europe — have most directly been touched by the reality of the world church is through music. That was never really planned by the World Council of Churches, and yet would not have happened without the WCC.

Most would point to the discovery and power of "ecumenical worship" at the WCC's Vancouver Assembly in 1983. The services in its worship tent captivated many of the participants. Subsequently, more intentional effort was put into the worship at WCC assemblies and other events. Eventually songs from the world church were compiled and became more available in resources like *Thuma Mina*[2] published by those in the German churches, but in German and English, in 1995. Participants at ecumenical events carried the music and worship they experienced back to their congregations.

---

2. *Thuma Mina: Singing with Our Partner Churches* (Basel: Basileia Verlag; Munich and Berlin: Strube Verlag, 1995).

Today it's not uncommon for songs from African, Latin American, and Asian settings to be sung in the worship of many congregations in the global North. It is one concrete way in which the global ecumenical movement has directly affected local congregations. But this should be a sign of a far deeper spiritual reality.

One cannot doubt evidence of a deep and growing hunger for expressions of Christian unity that move at a spiritual, experiential level, and bypass the dogmatic and institutional roadblocks otherwise standing in the way. One only need notice the extraordinary power of the Taizé community, and its global expressions, as it draws especially younger people into expressions of simple worship and community. Or witness the dramatic success of the Kirchentag in Germany, a festival of culture, causes, and worship drawing at least 100,000 a year. The Greenbelt Music Festival in England and more recently the Wild Goose Festival in the United States have similar characteristics.

Or consider the revival of the medieval traditions of pilgrimage, most notably to Santiago de Compostela, but also to the Nidaros Cathedral in Trondheim, Norway, where pilgrim pathways were officially reopened in 1997. Perhaps these and other emerging spiritual practices among many who are disenchanted with the institutionalized church are unexpected signs helping us seek our way forward.

As a signpost, this much seems clear. The pilgrim pathway of Christian unity should be undergirded by shared experiences of prayer, worship, and spiritual practices. These will, in fact, become major avenues for building trust, and being open to the surprising discoveries of God's grace and presence. As Pentecostals are deeply moved by Orthodox liturgy, and Catholics are inspired by powerful Protestant preaching, then we will begin to grasp how this pilgrimage together enriches all our own spiritual traditions.

4. United by Living Waters

What most wounds and damages the unity of the body of Christ as God's gift are exclusive ecclesiologies. These are the most daunting and injurious obstacles that our pilgrimage of Christian unity will face. While at one level we've always known this, it's been tempting to avoid this reality and to try to find our way around these stark and destructive barriers. Sometimes we live in polite denial of these painful realities.

But on this pathway, we've got to confront these truths honestly. When any denomination or communion defines itself over against other Christians as the only church that is true and pure, Christ's body is severed. Yet, this is what continues to happen today, over and over, among all traditions. With over 40,000 denominations, we now literally have thousands of versions of the true and pure church. It makes an utter and ludicrous mockery of our witness.

Even the Orthodox churches bear this burden. The churches of the Eastern Orthodox tradition and the Oriental Orthodox tradition still do not share communion together. Despite reconciling their intra-Orthodox theological differences, they have not taken the step that would welcome one another in full communion. And it seems out of the question, ecclesiologically, for Orthodox churches officially and theologically to regard a Protestant denomination as part of Christ's church.

When the Catholic Church instructs its young people and new members that they are to grow under the teaching and authority of the one true church, they draw an exclusive boundary between themselves and the other half of Christendom. When a group of displeased Presbyterians leave their denomination over ethical differences dealing with sexuality, and form another denomination, they are building a new wall of separation in Christ's unified body. When Pentecostal groups prohibit membership in a Christian ecumenical body with a string of accusations, they are self-righteously rejecting other parts of Christ's body as hopelessly contaminated by sin.

We don't like to speak this directly, but we should. And ironically, one reason why we can is that we have built up enough trust and healthy relationships to speak the truth with one another. But it's even deeper. Orthodox, Catholic, evangelical, Pentecostal, and Protestant believers who, in faithful obedience to their Lord, have been willing to walk on pilgrim pathways with one another come to know that the exclusive claims that their official ecclesiologies make, or that some of their leaders proclaim, simply don't reflect the truth and presence of God's Spirit in one another, which they have come to experience.

At some point, they reach a moment where they join with Peter, when he witnesses the presence of God's Spirit with the Gentiles and has to decide what that means: "If then God gave them the same gift that he gave us when we believed in the Lord Jesus Christ, who was I that I could hinder God?" (Acts 11:17).

Such a realization then motivates us to reexamine what our traditions have taught, or how creeds have been interpreted, in order to discover deeper dimensions of God's truth. This is why, even in the recognition of our differences, it's so important to commit ourselves to continue walking on this pilgrimage of Christian unity together. With one another, we build our relationships, share our stories, worship and pray, and then discover that "we were all made to drink of one Spirit" (1 Corinthians 12:13).

When we then turn to confront our exclusive ecclesiologies, the most fruitful way forward theologically is to consider our understanding of baptism. Here is where the fruits of theological dialogue come into play in ways that give us guidance in our pilgrimage. For example, the recently completed Reformed-Catholic dialogue in the United States, resulting in the common recognition of baptism, demonstrates how earnest exchanges can create important new realities.[3]

There's significant room to grow in how we understand these living waters, including the Pentecostal understandings of baptism of the Spirit. The foundational understanding of God's work through the Spirit in baptism, in my view, has the potential to appropriately question the exclusive character of various ecclesiologies. Within the Orthodox Church, for instance, practices around "rebaptism" vary. In some cases, when a person converts to the Orthodox Church after being baptized in another Christian tradition, rebaptism may not be required. Through baptism, a door can be opened to a fresh discussion on ecclesiology. And as previously mentioned, this has been the focus of the WCC's Faith and Order work over the last twenty years, resulting in the consensus document *The Church: Toward a Common Vision,* which will be featured at the Tenth Assembly in Busan. Ecclesiology is also the subject for the next round of dialogue between Reformed churches and the Catholic Church in the United States.

Walking together, with one another, we can find the grace to raise the honest questions of how our understandings of the body of Christ could ever exclude us from having fellowship with one another. In so doing, we may be turned onto a pathway of a unified understanding of the Spirit's presence and power in baptism, and what that means for our pilgrimage of Christian unity.

---

3. For full text see "These Living Waters: Common Agreement on Mutual Recognition of Baptism," on Reformed Church in America website at: http://images.rca.org/docs/synod/Synod2011-TheseLivingWaters.pdf.

5. A Missional Pilgrimage

A final signpost reminds us that this pilgrimage is not about ourselves. We are drawn into the unity that is God's gift to us in order to participate more fully in God's mission in the world. The phrase in Christ's prayer echoes again in our ears: "that the world may believe" (John 17:21).

We won't discover the unity of the body of Christ by sitting together; rather, this gift will come as we walk together. For this pilgrimage of Christian unity has both a purpose and a destination.

Our purpose is to participate together in God's mission in the world. This provides the missional motive to our thirst for living together as one. The work of God's Spirit in creating the body as one, and drawing us to live out of this reality, always has an outward dimension. We are sent, as one, into the world.

This reveals the nature of God's love. It is this self-giving love, fully expressed in Jesus Christ, that is poured into our hearts through the Spirit so that we may live in unity and love with one another. But this same love never turns in on itself. It always moves outward, to encompass, reconcile, and redeem what God has created.

Therefore, the pilgrimage of Christian unity walks in the way of God's mission. We see that in present experience. More and more, different churches, denominations, and Christian organizations are being drawn into deeper relationship with one another as they become more effectively engaged in the work of mission, evangelism, justice, and peace in the world.

Not only should we celebrate and expand these opportunities. We should also reflect on how they can lead us to discover deeper experiences of our unity with one another, overcoming the exclusive barriers that keep us sinfully divided. God's mission in the world is one. Through our pilgrimage, we will come to realize that this mission can never be fully realized through a church that persists in its sinful divisions.

A final dimension of this pilgrimage beckons us forward. In the prayer of Jesus in John 17, we read "The glory that you have given me I have given them, so that they may be one, as we are one" (John 17:22). Walking toward unity means walking into God's glory. The body together as one, in all its diversity, reflects fully the glory of God. And that is our destination. Our experience of being one is an expression of the fullness of the love and glory of the triune God.

As we travel toward that end, we will know we are on the way when we are creating space for new fellow pilgrims, listening deeply to each other's stories, singing together the Lord's song, celebrating the living water we share, and looking ahead to the horizon of God's mission.

CHAPTER EIGHT

Christians on the Move

The World Becomes Local

When the World Council of Churches' Central Committee, its governing body, meets in Geneva, members are housed in hotels near the Ecumenical Centre. A few years ago, when I was a member, we stayed at the Ramada Park Hotel. While the plenary sessions of the 150-member Central Committee were held at the Centre, various other committees and working groups met at the hotel. I would rent a car and drive to the plenary sessions, and after the meetings I would return to the hotel and find a parking space on the street two or three blocks away from the Ramada.

On one occasion, after returning from endless committee meetings dealing with budget deficits, structural reorganization proposals, reports of program activities, theological discussions on baptism, and urgent human rights conflicts around the world, I was walking wearily from my car to the hotel. Suddenly sounds of boisterous singing, music, and worship broke through this quiet, sedate Geneva neighborhood. It came from a community hall, a small building used for various functions and gatherings, just a block behind the Ramada. Curious, I wandered closer. A group of African immigrant Christians was engaged in a vibrant, spiritually exuberant worship service.

In cities throughout Europe and North America, thousands of congregations like these flourish today. Often, they are off of our ecclesiological radar even when they may be in the next block. My colleagues in the WCC, like me, had no idea that a group of African Christians were worshiping within a block of their comfortable hotel. Many would be surprised to learn that such congregations even existed in Geneva and elsewhere. They aren't identified on the ecumenical map.

At the same time, those African Christians who, through various pathways, found themselves in Geneva and gravitated to this congregation, gathering in a community hall in the northwestern part of the city off of Avenue Louis-Casal, could not imagine that the World Council of Churches was meeting a block away. More precisely, most would have little if any idea of what the World Council of Churches is, or that it exists to nurture Christian unity throughout the world.

That accidental encounter made a lasting impression on my ecumenical journey. At the time I knew little about the presence of such congregations, comprised of strangers and sojourners in cities like Geneva, and in New York, Chicago, and even Grand Rapids. As I walked away from that community hall into another WCC committee meeting in the hotel, I sensed moving from one religious world into another. Though a block apart, they were separated by a vast cultural, spiritual, and theological divide, and were unaware even of each other's existence. It was hard to know how to even think about building a bridge.

Yet, another impression began to form. The gap between the churches of the global North and those of the global South, which had become a focus of my work in ecumenical travels throughout the world, was immediately at hand, encountered when parking my car. These major divisions in world Christianity, experienced geographically, spiritually, and institutionally, were at our doorstep. Building a bridge between the churches of the global North, steeped in the tradition and catholicity of the Christian faith, and those of the global South, infused with a focused, contextual spiritual energy producing vital growth, could begin in the places I have called home — Chicago, Geneva, New York, and Grand Rapids.

Migration is transforming the religious life of Europe and North America. This has always been so, of course. Religious migrants have shaped the history of Christianity in the United States. But attention needs to be focused on how that reality is continuing today, in ways often not fully understood or appreciated. The influx of immigrants particularly since 1965 has made the United States the most religiously diverse country in the world.[1]

---

1. Jehu Hanciles, *Beyond Christendom: Globalization, African Migration, and the Transformation of the West* (Maryknoll, N.Y.: Orbis, 2008), p. 7.

Commonly we view immigration as introducing large numbers of non-Christian religions into U.S. society. Important scholars like Diana Eck have documented the fascinating increase in religious practice in the United States, particularly in her classic work, *A New Religious America*,[2] and in the Pluralism Project at Harvard University. Certainly stories abound about mosques springing up in cities once considered part of an American "Christendom." Grand Rapids, Michigan, a historic bulwark of Christian practice, education, and publishing, now has three mosques. In 2010, the number of mosques in the United States was 2,106, an increase from 1,209 a decade earlier.[3]

Buddhist religious practice seems almost commonplace in various regions. While accurate estimates of the number of Buddhists in the United States are difficult, they probably total between 1 and 2 percent of the population. But the United States is the top destination for the world's migrant Buddhists, including over half a million from Vietnam.

Hindu temples and retreat centers now appear throughout the American religious landscape. Immigration from Asian countries in recent decades also has dramatically increased the number of Hindus in the United States, including over 1 million from India, for a total U.S. Hindu population of about 2.29 million, which is still less than 1 percent of U.S. residents.[4]

Yet, popular assumptions about the impact of immigration on non-Christian religious practice in the United States disregard more fundamental realities. In fact, immigration to the United States is having its most dramatic religious effects on the Christian population of the country. That's because, first of all, an estimated 60 percent of all immigrants are Christian.[5] Moreover, many come with practices, traditions,

---

2. Diana L. Eck, *A New Religious America: How a "Christian Country" Has Now Become the World's Most Religiously Diverse Nation* (San Francisco: HarperSanFrancisco, 2001).

3. "Number of Mosques Up 74% since 2000," *USA Today*, February 29, 2012: http://usatoday30.usatoday.com/news/religion/story/2012-02-29/islamic-worship-growth-us/53298792/1.

4. "So, How Many Hindus Are There in the U.S.?" *Hinduism Today*, January/February/March 2008, p. 61. Also see David Briggs, "Hindu Americans: The Surprising, Hidden Population Trends of Hinduism in the U.S.," *The Huffington Post*, April 28, 2011: http://www.huffingtonpost.com/david-briggs/first-hindu-census-reveal_b_853758.html.

5. Hanciles, *Beyond Christendom*, p. 7.

and expressions of their faith that have been shaped in a non-Western context. They bring understandings and styles of Christian practice that often seem foreign to long-established traditions. As the introduction to a major study on religion and these new immigrants states, "Even though significant numbers of new immigrants are Christian, they are expressing their Christianity in languages, customs, and independent churches that are barely recognizable, and often controversial, for European-ancestry Catholics and Protestants."[6]

But these new Christian immigrants will have a dramatic effect on America's future religious life; in fact, their effect is already beginning to be experienced. Consider this. According to the 1990 census, 19.7 million people in the United States were born in another country.[7] By 2010, there were 43 million foreign-born residents in the United States, or one of out every five international migrants alive in the world. Of these, 74 percent were Christian, 5 percent were Muslim, 4 percent Buddhist, and 3 percent Hindu.[8] While those proportions will shift somewhat in the future, the overwhelming reality is that immigration to the United States is having a major effect on the Christian population in the country. A strong argument can be made, for instance, that the growing percentage of those who classify themselves as having no religious affiliation in the United States — now at 20 percent — would be higher were it not for immigration.

Not surprisingly, the greatest number of immigrants living in the United States come from Mexico, totaling 12.9 million, 95 percent of whom are Christian. The Philippines provides the second largest number, totaling 1.8 million, nearly all of whom are Christian. India follows with 1.6 million people resident in the United States but born in India; 45 percent of them are Hindu, 27 percent are Muslim, and 19 percent are Christian. Out of 1.1 million immigrants from El Salvador, 1 million are Christian. Christians from the Dominican Republic that live in the

---

6. Helen Rose Fuchs Ebaugh and Janet Stalzman Chafetz, *Religion and the New Immigrants: Continuities and Adaptations in Immigrant Congregations* (Walnut Creek, Calif.: AltaMira, 2000), p. 14.

7. Ebaugh and Chafetz, *Religion and the New Immigrants,* p. 13.

8. This information is found in the Global Migration and Religion Database, a project of the Pew Forum on Religion and Public Life. An interpretative article, "Faith on the Move: The Religious Affiliation of International Migrants," was released on March 8, 2012, and can be found at: http://www.pewforum.org/geography/religious-migration -exec.aspx.

United States number 740,000, along with 700,000 Christians from Guatemala and 860,000 Christians from Cuba.[9]

An estimated 214 million people in the world today are migrants, living in a country different from where they were born. Nearly half of these migrants are Christians — about 105 million, far more than the proportion of Christians in the world, which is about 33 percent. And for these Christians who are on the move, the United States is their chief destination; they presently account for about 32 million, or 13 percent of the Christian community in the United States. That percentage will continue to rise. These new immigrant Christians are changing America's religious landscape. Despite the growing religious pluralism in the United States, the dramatic, ongoing story of religious migration to this country will be revealed keenly in the contours of American Christianity.

Not only do the numbers of these Christian migrants to the United States tell this story. It's also the intensity of their belief and religious practice. Jehu Hanciles, a native of Sierra Leone who now is chair of World Christianity at the Candler School of Theology in Atlanta, and previously taught at Fuller Seminary in Pasadena, California, has done pioneering studies of non-Western Christianity. His book *Beyond Christendom: Globalization, African Migration, and the Transformation of the West* is a masterful, deeply researched presentation focusing particularly on the effects of South-North migration, and the missiological significance of African migration to the United States. The life and witness of seventy African immigrant congregations in six U.S. cities are also examined. At one point Hanciles observes: "Certainly, the vigorous growth of immigrant churches and congregations in metropolitan centers throughout the country over the last three to four decades suggests that they represent the most dynamic and thriving centers of Christian faith in America."[10]

The New African Diaspora

Hanciles observes "that every Christian migrant is a potential missionary."[11] Indeed, many African Christians drawn to the United States for a

9. All these figures are also from "Faith on the Move," which features interactive maps with multiple and rich resources of information.

10. Hanciles, *Beyond Christendom*, p. 286.

11. Hanciles, *Beyond Christendom*, p. 6.

variety of reasons come with a missionary mind-set, reflective of the congregations that have nurtured their faith. While immigrants from Africa to the United States constitute a modest share of the country's foreign-born residents (3.9 percent in 2009), the growth of this community has been striking. In 1960, when John F. Kennedy, who coined the phrase "a nation of immigrants," was inaugurated as president, 35,355 African-born residents were living in the United States. Fifty years later, that number had increased forty-fold, to 1.5 million.[12] The African countries with the greatest number of emigrants to the United States have been Nigeria, Ethiopia, Egypt, Ghana, and Kenya. Of these, 210,000 Christians have emigrated from Nigeria, 90,000 Christians both from Ethiopia and Egypt, 110,000 Christians from Ghana, and 70,000 from Kenya.[13] Many bring non-Western expressions of Christianity nurtured in the soil of Africa.

A decade ago I struck up a conversation with Rufus Ositelu, primate of the Church of the Lord (Aladura), during a meeting of the WCC Central Committee. I knew almost nothing about his church. He had shared with me that he had been working as a computer expert in Germany but had been called to the position of primate of his church, headquartered in Nigeria.

As we talked together on a pleasant day in Geneva at the beginning of September, Rufus told me he had just recently come from a special time of retreat, with prayer and fasting, held each year. The primate explained that the leadership of the church gathers together, and no major decisions are made without this special period of prayer. Further, he said that at the end of this period, the members of the church are invited to come and join this experience of retreat and prayer.

I was intrigued. In my role as general secretary of the Reformed Church in America, I had become convinced that we needed to find new methods of discernment and decision making that moved beneath and beyond the typical format of tightly structured assemblies ruled by parliamentary procedures. Anxious to learn more, I asked Primate Ositelu how many people from the church at large joined for the conclusion of this retreat.

---

12. Kristen McCabe, "African Immigrants in the United States," *Migration Information Source,* July 2011, published by the Migration Policy Institute: http://www.migra tioninformation.org/feature/display.cfm?ID=847.

13. "Faith on the Move."

He replied, "About one million."

Suddenly I realized I was talking with the leader of a church whose scope and ministry were beyond anything I had imagined. And despite my ecumenical experience and the unique participation of this church in the WCC, I was unaware, to my regret, of the richness represented by this remarkable expression of the body of Christ.

Following a pattern similar to other member bodies of the African Instituted Churches, the Church of the Lord (Aladura) was founded in 1930 by the Prophet Joshua Ositelu in Ogere-Remo, Nigeria. ("Aladura," in Yoruba, means "Prayer Fellowship," or "the Praying People.") He was twenty-eight years old at the time. Originally studying to be an Anglican minister, his spiritual experiences resulted in severing his ties with the colonial church. He went to a place in Ogere to fast and pray, and received revelations. He named the place Mount Tabborrar, and it became a site for an annual pilgrimage of believers for days of prayer, fasting, healing, and renewal, held each August. This was the experience Primate Rufus Ositelu had just completed about seventy years later, and was sharing with me in Geneva.

The four tenets of the church are described as "Pentecostal in Power, Biblical in Pattern, Evangelical in Ministry, Ecumenical in Outlook."[14] The last is particularly significant and unique for African Instituted Churches, making this church a member of the WCC and other ecumenical bodies in countries where their congregations are found. The church has grown to 3.6 million members, not only throughout Nigeria, but also in neighboring African countries such as Liberia, as well as in Great Britain, Germany, and the United States.

The Church of the Lord (Aladura) is one of thousands of such churches belonging to the Organization of African Instituted Churches (AIC). The organization represents 60 million Christians in denominations and congregations throughout the continent and in the African diaspora. Totally independent from the church structures of Western mission, churches in the AIC forged indigenous expressions of Christian faith, often in opposition to the harsh and controlling forces of colonial rule. With colonialism's demise, these churches flourished.

While exhibiting wide diversity rooted in their various approaches to the contextualization of their faith in African culture, churches in the

14. See the website of the Church of the Lord (Aladura): http://aladura.info/Our_History.html.

AIC share some common characteristics. Some helpful observations come from David Shank, a Mennonite missionary who began encounters with these churches in 1971, and then served as a teacher of Scripture for ten years at the invitation of the African Instituted Churches in Cote d'Ivoire (Ivory Coast), from 1979 to 1989. Writing on what those in the West can learn from African Instituted Churches, he lists these insights:

1. The faith of the powerful is irrelevant.
2. The gospel is the source of liberating power.
3. Faith is spiritual combat.
4. The Western interpretation of Scripture is not the final word.
5. God is experienced as an awe-inspiring mystery.
6. The power of the faith community is in the laity.[15]

Increasingly, churches of the AIC are finding homes within the United States as the migration of Christians from Africa has rapidly escalated in recent decades. Those churches are joined by Christian immigrants from traditional Protestant denominations in Africa, such as the Presbyterian Church in Ghana, the Methodist Church in Sierra Leone, and countless others. But these Christians as well bring textures of their traditions deeply shaped by African culture.

Nowhere have the stories of such congregations been told more vividly than in *Word Made Global,* by Mark R. Gornik.[16] To focus the impact of African Christianity in New York City, Gornik relates in depth the stories of three African migrant congregations that he studied extensively for five years: the Redeemed Christian Church of God International Chapel, in Brooklyn; the Presbyterian Church of Ghana, in Harlem; and the Church of the Lord (Aladura), in the Bronx.

Gornik tells in illuminating ways the stories of their ministerial

---

15. James R. Krabill, ed., *Mission from the Margins: Selected Writings from the Life and Ministry of David A. Shank* (Elkhart, Ind.: Institute of Mennonite Studies, 2010). Shank wrote a doctoral dissertation on the life and thought of William Wade Harris, the founder of the Harrist Church, a major body of the AIC in Francophone Africa. The entire history of the Mennonite Church's relationship with the AIC is fascinating. Beginning in 1959, North American Mennonites began a process leading to relationships with a wide number of churches in the AIC in ten different African countries.

16. Mark R. Gornik, *Word Made Global: Stories of African Christianity in New York City* (Grand Rapids: Eerdmans, 2011).

calling and formation, their worship life, their deep spirituality, their ministries, and their sense of missionary vocation, and suggests broader lessons and conclusions for the impact of African congregations on American Christianity. Supported by meticulous research, this is a hallmark contribution, pioneering in examining congregations so often neglected in the study of religious life in the United States. If you live in one of the major urban areas of the United States, it's likely that there's a congregation belonging to the African Instituted Churches near you.

Unintended Ecclesiological Consequences

In 1965, President Lyndon Johnson stood at the Statue of Liberty and signed the Immigration and Naturalization Act, called the Hart-Celler Act, a major reform of U.S. immigration law. At the signing ceremony, however, he said, "This bill that we will sign today is not a revolutionary bill. It does not affect the lives of millions."[17] The president could not have been more mistaken.

Up until that time, immigration policy in the United States was based on a national origins quota system that in retrospect could only be called blatantly racist. Of those entering the United States, 82 percent were from northern and western Europe. Africans and Asians were excluded, and southern European immigration was severely limited. In the era of the civil rights movement, new attention was focused on how our immigration laws contradicted the principles of equality enshrined in the nation's founding.

But other motives were in play, including the desire to increase immigration from other regions of Europe, such as Greece and Italy, a cause embraced by the Democratic Party. The new law eliminated race and national origin as bases for immigration, intending to put all nations on an equal footing. Quotas were established — 170,000 for the Western Hemisphere and 120,000 for the Eastern Hemisphere. The law also placed a priority on the reuniting of families as well as on admitting those with needed skills.

No one, it's fair to say, envisioned the consequences. In pressing for

17. President Johnson's remarks can be found at: http://www.lbjlib.utexas.edu/ johnson/archives.hom/speeches.hom/651003.asp.

passage of immigration reform, political pressures combined with commonly accepted assumptions, and politicians downplayed its potential effects. Robert Kennedy, as attorney general, gave this assurance to a House subcommittee: "I would say for the Asia-Pacific Triangle it [immigration] would be approximately 5,000, Mr. Chairman, after which immigration from that source would virtually disappear; 5,000 immigrants would come the first year, but we do not expect that there would be any great influx after that."[18]

In fact, the 1965 act was a watershed in Asian immigration, as well as opening up the flow of nonwhite immigrants from Latin America, Africa, and the Caribbean. The provision for uniting families had a particularly strong effect on Asian immigration. In 1965, the Asian American population in the United States was about .05 percent of the total. By 2002, 7.3 million Asians had arrived in the United States, significantly exceeding Robert Kennedy's estimate.

Provisions allowing for needed skills also produced unexpected consequences. As sociologist Stephen Klineberg said, "It never occurred to anyone, literally, that there were going to be African doctors, Indian engineers, Chinese computer programmers who'd be able, for the first time in the 20th century, to immigrate to America."[19]

According to 2010 U.S. Census data, 17.3 million Asian Americans now are residents of the United States, constituting 5.6 percent of the population; 50 percent of those over the age of twenty-five have at least a bachelor's degree, compared to 28 percent of the overall population that age. In the last decade, the Asian American population grew by 46 percent, a faster rate than any other racial group. The Census Bureau estimates this group will grow to 40 million by 2050.[20]

The Christian community in the United States has been notably affected by this influx of Asian immigrants. While the Census Bureau does not compile data on religious affiliation of such racial groups, sociologists have evaluated data from various surveys. One sociologist of religion, Jerry Park, doing a major evaluation in 2009 looking at various

18. U.S. Congress, House Hearings, 1964, p. 418, cited in a 1995 study on the thirtieth anniversary of the bill, found at: http://www.cis.org/articles/1995/back395.html.

19. From 2006 report on National Public Radio by Jennifer Ludden. See http://www.npr.org/templates/story/story.php?storyId=5391395.

20. U.S. Census Bureau, "Facts for Features: Asian/Pacific American Heritage Month: May 2011," April 29, 2011: http://www.census.gov/newsroom/releases/archives/facts_for_features_special_editions/cb11-ff06.html.

surveys, indicated that 44 percent of all Asian Americans are Christian. Of these, 43.3 percent are evangelical Protestant, 17.1 percent are mainline Protestant, and 36.6 percent are Catholic.[21]

The Korean American community, totaling some 1.7 million, is estimated to be about 80 percent Christian, compared to about 30-40 percent of the population in Korea. Many Korean immigrants arriving as non-Christians are converted. The prayerful power of Korean congregations is well known, with numbers of Korean congregations growing in mainline and evangelical Christian denominations. Others are in Baptist churches, remain independent, or are part of denominations comprised of Korean congregations in the United States, such as the Korean Presbyterian Church in America.

The growth of the church in Korea, as mentioned earlier, has marked it apart from Christianity in most other parts of that continent. One factor contributing to that growth was the opposition of many Korean Christians to Japanese occupation, and their struggle for Korean independence. When visiting churches in Korea, I have seen the spiritual regard for the "blood of the martyrs" who resisted Japanese colonialism. One can reflect on similarities to the colonial resistance of the African Instituted Churches, and their subsequent growth.

Christian immigrants from the Philippines and Vietnam are having noticeable effects on the U.S. Catholic Church. While Asians still constitute only about 1 percent of Catholics in the country, a survey in 2005 reported that they accounted for 13 percent of those studying for the priesthood, and most of these were Vietnamese.[22] Of the 1.1 million Vietnamese living in the United States, 350,000 are Christian, and most of these are Catholic.[23] Among Filipinos who have come to the United States, 68 percent are Catholic and 18 percent are Protestant.[24]

---

21. Jerry Z. Park, "Assessing the Sociological Study of Asian American Christianity," *Society of Asian North American Christianity Studies Journal*, 2009, 57-94. Park uses a PNAAPS survey from 2001 for a table on page 60 of this article, but compares this to later surveys as well. A blog by Park, "Surveying Religion in Asian America," written on November 4, 2011, briefly summarizes three major surveys, all with similar results: http://www.patheos.com/blogs/blackwhiteandgray/2011/11/surveying-religion-in-asian-america/.

22. Neela Banerjee, "Clergy's Call Still Strong for Young Vietnamese," *New York Times*, December 11, 2005.

23. "Faith on the Move."

24. Park, "Assessing the Sociological Study," p. 60.

The largest group of Asian Americans are of Chinese decent, comprising 3.8 million people.[25] An estimated 23 percent are Christian (20 percent Protestant and 3 percent Catholic).[26] What is interesting for this community, however, is the pattern of Chinese immigrants who are converted through existing Chinese American churches. Given the rapid growth of Christianity in China, the pattern of the future movement of people between China and the United States could have important consequences. For Taiwanese Christians, the pattern is the same. While Christians constitute only about 4.5 percent of the population in Taiwan, 25-30 percent of Taiwanese in the United States are Christians, with estimates that as many as two-thirds are converts.[27]

These dynamics are seen among international students in the United States. In 2011, 723,000 students from abroad were studying in the country, and 60 percent of those were from Asia. Among that group, 157,000 were from China.[28] Frequently, these visiting students are welcomed by Chinese American churches and by Chinese and Asian Christian fellowship groups on campuses. Such hospitality, which is a New Testament practice that is now central amidst the changing patterns of migration, often leads to conversion as one joins this community of faith, gathering fellow sojourners in a new land.

Overall, evangelical collegiate groups such as InterVarsity now witness large numbers of Asian American students who participate, and in some cases predominate, in local chapters. This includes some of the most prestigious universities in the United States, such as Stanford and Harvard.[29] And in turn, those effects already are being felt in U.S. seminaries. Fuller Theological Seminary, for instance, reported that of its 5,000 students, 1,100 were Asian citizens or Asian Americans.[30]

Asian American Christians, with their high levels of education and

25. U.S. Census Bureau, "Facts for Features."

26. Park, "Assessing the Sociological Study," p. 60.

27. Hanciles, *Beyond Christendom*, p. 297. Hanciles actually states that Taiwan's Christian population is 2 percent, but other estimates, such as the CIA's public World Factbook, place this figure at 4.5 percent.

28. From a talk given by Joel Carpenter, "World Christianity Right Here," to the Commission on Christian Unity of the Reformed Church in America on October 12, 2012. Dr. Carpenter is director of the Nagel Institute for the Study of World Christianity at Calvin College in Grand Rapids, Michigan.

29. Tim Stafford, "The Tiger in the Academy," *Christianity Today,* April 2006, pp. 70-73.

30. Stafford, "Tiger in the Academy," p. 73.

deeply rooted spirituality, will have a growing impact on Christianity in the United States, as this racial group grows at a faster rate than any other in the country.

The Meshing of Civilizations

In 1968, while a graduate student in theology at Princeton Seminary, I had a conversation with one of my favorite professors, Dr. James Billington. An expert on Russian history and culture, he taught at Princeton's Woodrow Wilson School of Public and International Affairs. I asked Dr. Billington what area of study I might consider that would have a major effect on the future trends of history, and the evolution of our democracy. Dr. Billington identified the role of Spanish culture and civilization. He thought that the rising significance of Latin America, its proximity to the United States, and the increasing interplay of cultures through immigration and other means could have a decisive influence on our future. Yet, so much about Hispanic culture was not studied, understood, and appreciated.

Dr. Billington's comments reminded me of similar observations made by Dr. John MacKay, who served as president of Princeton Theological Seminary from 1936 until 1959. Prior to that, MacKay had been a missionary, helping lead a school in Lima, Peru, at a time of reform movements in Latin America. He also became a key figure in the ecumenical movement. I recall being told by my Young Life leader and mentor, Bill Starr, that Dr. MacKay was predicting that the cultural, political, and religious life of the United States would be profoundly impacted by our Hispanic neighbors, and we were unaware and unprepared for this encounter.

Dr. Billington, now Librarian of the Congress, and Dr. MacKay, who was a professor of Hispanic thought at American University following his time at Princeton, and died in 1983, were both prescient in their observations. In the last four decades, no "foreign" civilization has had a greater impact on U.S. society than Hispanic culture. We've witnessed a meshing of civilizations, filled with tensions and conflicts, as well as creativity and promise, that continues to this day.

Hispanics, either foreign born or by ancestry, now total 50 million people in the United States. Almost 33 million are from Mexico; 4.8 million are from Puerto Rico; El Salvador, the Dominican Republic, Cuba, and Guatemala each account for between 1 million and 2 million residents.[31] Of the estimated 11.2 million unauthorized residents in the United States, about 80 percent are Hispanic.[32]

The influx of Mexicans to the United States over the past four decades, bringing 12 million new residents to this country, has been unprecedented in our history for a movement of people from any single country. Slightly over half are unauthorized residents.[33] Yet, the startling fact is that net immigration from Mexico to the United States has halted, and may even be reversing itself. The recession in the United States, combined with increased border enforcement, a high level of deportations under the Obama administration, and improving economic conditions in Mexico, has resulted in as many, if not more, Mexicans leaving the United States than entering.[34]

Yet, Mexican American and overall Hispanic populations are intrinsic features of American society that will continue to grow and shape our future. Between 2000 and 2010, birthrates in the United States accounted for 63 percent of the increase in the population of Mexican Americans, larger than immigration during that period.[35] So, while the rate of Asian American immigration has recently surpassed that of Hispanics, the Latino population of the United States will continue to increase substantially from the present 50 million.

About 70 percent of the Hispanic population in the United States

31. Pew Hispanic Center, from 2012 American Community Survey: http://www.pew hispanic.org/.

32. Jeffrey Pasal and D'Vera Cohn, "Unauthorized Immigrant Population, National and State Trends, 2010," *Pew Hispanic Center,* February 1, 2011: http://www.pewhis panic.org/2011/02/01/ii-current-estimates-and-trends/.

33. Jeffrey Pasal, D'Vera Cohn, and Ana Gonzales-Barrera, "Net Migration from Mexico Falls to Zero, and Perhaps Less," *Pew Hispanic Center,* May 3, 2012: http://www .pewhispanic.org/2012/04/23/net-migration-from-mexico-falls-to-zero-and-perhaps-less/. While the sheer number of Mexican immigrants in this period is larger than any other influx in U.S. history, if measured as a proportion of immigration to the United States, the waves of nineteenth-century immigration from Germany and Ireland are similar, if not greater, according to the authors.

34. Pasal, Cohn, and Gonzales-Barrera, "Net Migration from Mexico Falls to Zero." However, some recent studies indicate that improving economic conditions in the United States during 2012 may be resulting in a slight increase of illegal immigration from Mexico. See "Improved Economy Draws Migrants," *USA Today,* October 26-28, 2012, p. 1.

35. "The Mexican-American Boom: Births Overtake Immigration," *Pew Hispanic Center,* July 14, 2011: http://www.pewhispanic.org/2011/07/14/the-mexican-american-boom -brbirths-overtake-immigration/.

is Catholic. And about 35 percent of the U.S. Catholic community is now Hispanic. That figure will continue to rise. Hispanics are dramatically reshaping the nature and texture of Catholicism in the United States, particularly in cities and regions with high Hispanic populations. In Los Angeles, for example, an estimated 70 percent of Catholics are Hispanic.[36]

It's critical to realize that Hispanic Catholics have their own contextualized practices of their faith. Not only is that reflected in images of the Virgin of Guadalupe throughout Mexican neighborhoods in U.S. cities. Their forms of Catholic piety reflect the inculturation of Christianity in Latin America. Moreover, it is estimated that 54 percent of Latino Catholics identify themselves as charismatic, and thus incorporate the practices of spiritual healing, speaking in tongues, and gifts of the Holy Spirit common in Pentecostal circles.[37]

About 23 percent of Latinos, however, are Protestant, accounting for a sizable 9.5 million Christians in the United States.[38] There are more Latino Protestants in the United States than Episcopalians. The great majority of these are Pentecostal or evangelical — about 85 percent, according to the National Hispanic Christian Leadership Conference. Many can be found in the thousands of storefront churches and chapels that dot Hispanic neighborhoods in large U.S. urban areas. Some affiliate with existing U.S denominations, at times wishing to preserve their Pentecostal style of worship and practice, but seeking forms of association, theology, and church polity that guard against the extreme independence and excesses of charismatic pastoral leaders.

While stressing intense personal spiritual experiences and the direct divine intervention of God's power in human affairs, along with traditionally conservative views of theology and morality, Hispanic Christians — both Catholic and Protestant — bring expressions of faith that are formed and shaped by their original culture. These don't disappear, but rather become part of how they shape their identity within their new land. Further, forms of social solidarity and action, especially around the issues of immigration and justice, often find strong expression within the Hispanic Christian community.

36. Hanciles, *Beyond Christendom*, p. 294.
37. Hanciles, *Beyond Christendom*, p. 295.
38. Bruce Murray, "Latino Religion in the U.S.: Demographic Shifts and Trend," National Hispanic Christian Leadership Conference website: http://www.nhclc.org/news/latino-religion-us-demographic-shifts-and-trend.

Across most of the spectrum of Christianity in the United States, Hispanic believers are having deep effects on worship, practice, and witness. Over 4,000 Catholic parishes now have a Hispanic ministry, and Hispanics have constituted 71 percent of the growth of U.S. Catholics since 1960.[39] But the Protestant world as well is experiencing the rising influence of Latinos, with their frequent combination of evangelical theology, Pentecostal style, and social justice commitments. Emerging groups like the National Latino Evangelical Coalition, led by Rev. Gabriel Salguero, and National Hispanic Christian Leadership have gained recognition and influence in the U.S. political landscape. As the Hispanic community is projected to grow to 106 million by 2050, their presence will become one of the defining features of American Christianity.

A Non-Western Missionary Movement

Global trends will ensure that migration, particularly from the South to the North as well as from the East to the West, will be a growing part of the world's future. In this world the richest 1 percent receive income equal to that of the poorest 57 percent. Economic conditions as well as social conflicts will continue to produce pressure for people to migrate, as possible, from relatively impoverished to more affluent countries. Some have no choice but to be on the move, fleeing persecution or war. Others seek temporary sojourns for educational or employment opportunities. Many more make permanent new homes.

Within the more economically disadvantaged societies of the global South, the vast proportion of the world's population growth will take place — half in Asia, and a third in Africa.[40] Eighty percent of the world's population is found in Africa, Asia, Latin America, and the Caribbean. Meanwhile, population growth in the developed world has stagnated, and demands for labor in those societies increase. Thus, the global movement of people from South to North, and East to West, will be an increasing trend in the world.

39. "Hispanic Catholics in the United States," backgrounder, prepared by the U.S. Conference of Catholic Bishops: http://www.usccb.org/issues-and-action/cultural-diversity/upload/hispanic-catholics.pdf.

40. Jehu Hanciles, "Migration and Mission: The Religious Significance of the North South Divide," in *Mission in the 21st Century,* ed. Andrew Walls and Cathy Ross (Maryknoll, N.Y.: Orbis, 2008), p. 123.

Further, the majority of those on the move will continue to be Christian. And if, in fact, every Christian migrant is a potential missionary, we are witnessing a major, non-Western missionary movement in the world. Think of it this way. As the West becomes post-Christian, non-Western Christianity is coming to the West.

Jehu Hanciles puts it this way: "First, attentiveness to the nature and composition of human migration is crucial for understanding the possibilities and the potential of Christian missionary endeavor; second . . . in much the same way that the Western missionary movement proved decisive for the current shape of global Christianity the future of global Christianity is now intricately bound up with the emerging non-Western missionary."[41]

How existing congregations in societies shaped and molded by Western Christianity, and now becoming increasingly secularized, respond to Christian immigrants now living in their midst will be decisive for the future shape of Christian witness. Even more, this is where the major divisions of world Christianity, which now tear the members of the global body of Christ asunder, and keep them in isolation from one another, can find a hope of healing, and a rediscovery of the unity given as God's gift. As in the past, when the modern ecumenical movement has its beginning, a fresh and discerning understanding of how God's mission is working in the world today can be the portal for grasping anew the radical, demanding, but life-giving call to Christian unity.

41. Hanciles, "Migration and Mission," p. 129.

CHAPTER NINE

Word Becoming Flesh, Congregationally

Singing a New Song

The St. Olaf College Choir is recognized as probably the finest collegiate choir performing sacred choral music in the country. The college is located in Northfield, Minnesota, and reflects the heritage of Norwegian immigrants, who founded the institution. A century ago, in 1912, the choir was founded by F. Melius Christiansen, and emerged to become a premier a cappella choral group, setting a standard in performance excellence.

The St. Olaf Christmas Festival, featuring seven various choirs of the college, is regularly televised nationally and internationally. Twenty-five CDs have been produced from these events, as well as other choral music. The choir's CD *Great Hymns of the Faith* has sold over 270,000 copies. Since 1990, Dr. Anton Armstrong has been the conductor of the St. Olaf Choir. The choir has performed on tours both throughout the United States and internationally.

Listening to the annual St. Olaf Christmas concert is a highlight of the season for my wife and me. Their various Christmas CDs fill our home with music throughout the season. But listening to the choir over the past couple of decades, under Dr. Armstrong's leadership, I noticed a change in the diversity of its music. While classic choral pieces, both ancient and modern, have always been featured, and music inspired by the African American community has for long been part of its repertoire, more recent years have seen Christian music from various countries and cultures anchored in the global South.

In 1996 we heard "Natufurahi Siku Ya Leo" by Boniface Mganga.

"Freedom Is Coming" is a South African song that was included the year before. The album *Hallelujah! We Sing Your Praises,* one of our favorites, includes "Haleluya! Pelo Tsa Roma," also from South Africa, among others. "An African Noel" was performed in 2003, "Betelehemu" in 2006, and "Oba Se Je," a Nigerian folk song, in the 2009 Christmas festival.

For many Christians in the global North, the awareness of world Christianity and its presence in our own cultural and spiritual environment come through song. Earlier I mentioned how music first shared at World Council of Churches assemblies from Christian traditions around the world has begun to find its way into the singing of some congregations in the global North. But the featuring of musical pieces from churches in Zimbabwe and Nigeria in events like the St. Olaf Christmas Festival breaks traditional expectations of Bach, Handel, Robert Scholz, and John Rutter in startling ways. Even the cherished celebrations of the birth of Jesus depart in song from the normalcy of the past. And when better than Christmas, as we remember that the Word becomes flesh.

Thus, often we hear the songs of those from foreign lands before we see and meet the ones whose tongues first sang them. But at some point, the movement of millions throughout the world, both non-Christian and Christian, who are crossing boundaries, and coming to new lands such as the United States, comes into contact with congregations well established in the soil and culture of America. It is there, in the flesh-and-blood realities of local congregations, with their wounds, wonderings, and witness, that the incarnation faces an empirical test. What does it mean, in this time, place, and space, to say we belong to one body?

Tip O'Neill, the longtime Speaker of the House of Representatives, famously said that all politics is local. Perhaps we could say today that all ecclesiology is local. Not that we deny, of course, the mystery of belonging to "one holy catholic church." But in today's world, perhaps more than ever, and more as it was in the first two Christian centuries, if that belonging does not become incarnate locally, in the specificity of congregations, it may be meaningless.

Welcoming the Stranger

One of the most well known and revered icons today was painted by Andrei Rublev between 1422 and 1425 in Russia, and is a reflection on "The Holy Trinity." The original is in the Tretiakov Gallery in Moscow, but reproductions abound, not only in Orthodox circles but also among Protestants and Catholics, and in ecumenical settings.

The icon depicts three angels, messengers of God, seated around a table, bearing a chalice. The female figures form a circle evoking deep mutuality, interconnectedness, and love between one another. But the circle is open, inviting the world into this profound experience of community. As Christine Challiot, an Eastern Orthodox laywoman, wrote, "Rublev painted the three angels with a circular motion to signify their unity and equality, 'thus creating a unity to represent the Holy Trinity in its movement of love.'"[1]

A copy of this icon hangs in a hallway in the Ecumenical Centre in Geneva. Small reproductions are plentiful, and the late Henri Nouwen, a friend, gave one to my daughter Karis when she was born. She still treasures it today. Orthodox offer deeply moving theological reflections on the meaning of the Trinity based on this icon. Feminist theologians are drawn to it because they see female images depicting the Trinity. You can buy a high quality, 18" x 24" print online for $49.99 at Art.com.

But this profound reflection on the Trinity comes in the biblical context of giving hospitality to the stranger. The icon depicts the story of the hospitality offered by Abraham and Sarah in Genesis 18:1-15. Having followed God's call, Abraham and Sarah were at their home, a tent on the plain in Mamre. Three strangers came by. Abraham rushed to offer them hospitality, bringing water, and then cakes made by Sarah, plus milk, and then a calf was prepared to share.

But the three migrating strangers, in fact, are messengers of God. The text says simply that they were the Lord; interpreters see the three as the presence of the Trinity. And they, in turn, bring an announcement that Sarah, in her old age, will bear a son, fulfilling God's promises. Sarah and Abraham suddenly find the tables reversed, and they are the guests at God's table, being invited into this community of love. Thus, in reflecting on Rublev's icon, Catholic theologian Elizabeth Johnson explains, "This is a depiction of a Trinitarian God capable of immense hospitality who calls the world to join the feast."[2]

---

1. Christine Challiot, "Contemplating Rublev's Icon: The Authority of the Trinity and the Community of Men and Women in the Church," *Ecumenical Review* 60, no. 1/2 (January/April 2008): 138; interior quotation is from E. Sendler, *The Icon: Image of the Invisible* (Torrance, Calif.: Oakwood Publications, 1993), p. 74.

2. Elizabeth A. Johnson, "Trinity: To Let the Symbol Sign Again," *Theology Today* 54 (October 1997): 299.

The biblical story presented in Rublev's moving icon is a declaration of the unexpected, life-giving presence of God, discovered in the context of providing hospitality to strangers.[3] That obligation is persistent in the Hebrew Scriptures. Rabbi Jonathan Sacks, for instance, notes that the love of strangers is declared thirty-six times in those Scriptures, as opposed to the love of neighbor, mentioned only once.[4] The love of strangers and sojourners in the Hebrew Scriptures is a primary test of one's love for God, and this is linked to the presence of migrating people, with whom we can unexpectedly encounter God in fresh and promising ways that open the future to new possibilities.

Patrick Keifert perceptively pointed this out two decades ago in *Welcoming the Stranger:* "Over a period of 1,500 years, no matter where the people of Israel were located, their worship was focused on the stranger; indeed, the prophets were critical of Israel whenever it failed to reserve a place for the stranger."[5] The imperative of compassion and inclusion for the stranger and alien in their midst was rooted in the nature of God's love, and in Israel's memory that it lived as an exile in a strange land: "When an alien resides with you in your land, you shall not oppress the alien. The alien who resides with you shall be to you as the citizen among you; you shall love the alien as yourself, for you were aliens in the land of Egypt: I am the LORD your God" (Leviticus 19:33-34).

This intrinsic connection between the experience of God's love and the stance toward the stranger, alien, and those from a different cultural background resounds through the life and ministry of Jesus. With his parents, of course, Jesus began his life as a refugee, part of an exiled, migrant family in Egypt, echoing the experience of the people of Israel. Then, the movement of reaching across borders and boundaries that constricted the understanding of God's love became a constant pattern in both the parables and the actions of Jesus.

One of the few times when Jesus speaks of judgment, in Matthew 25, he focuses on his presence in the midst of the marginalized. In that lit-

---

3. See Miguel H. Diaz, "On Loving Strangers: Encountering the Mystery of God in the Face of Migrants," *Word and World* 29, no. 3 (Summer 2009): 234-42. Diaz's article makes a direct connection between Rublev's icon and the call to welcome strangers in the context of immigration. Born in Cuba, and formerly a Catholic professor of theology at St. John's University in Minnesota, Diaz was appointed by President Barack Obama as U.S. ambassador to the Vatican in 2009.

4. Quoted in Diaz, "On Loving Strangers," p. 237.

5. Patrick R. Keifert, *Welcoming the Stranger* (Minneapolis: Fortress, 1992), p. 59.

any of failure to demonstrate compassion and show justice, the imperatives given to the people of Israel echo again: "I was a stranger and you did not welcome me" (25:43). This extended directly to the early church's initial understanding of following Jesus and belonging to the body of Christ. As William O'Neill writes,

> Christian hospitality to "strangers and aliens" shaped the earliest understanding of disciples as fellow "citizens with the saints" in the "household of God" (Eph 2:19). Indeed, hospitality (*philoxenia,* "love of the stranger") is at the very heart of Christian discipleship. . . . Again and again in the image of the eschatological feast (Amos 9:13-15; Joel 3:18; Isa 25:6-8), hospitality is offered not only to kin and kind, but also to those whose only claim is vulnerability and need (Matt 8:11; 22:1-14; Luke 14:12-14).[6]

The increase in migration to the United States, and the presence of 11.2 million who are not legally authorized to be in the country, has raised attention to the biblical, theological, and moral issues at stake for U.S. Christians and congregations. Recent years have seen several books and many articles exploring these themes in rich ways.[7] A broad ecumenical consensus has been developed with evangelical, Catholic, and mainline Protestant voices underscoring how biblical imperatives conflict sharply with present political realities. (Orthodox voices, while less visible, have also been involved as part of efforts carried out by the National Council of Churches.)

The National Association of Evangelicals and even the Southern Baptist Convention have joined in efforts at immigration reform that had been championed earlier, in some cases, by mainline Protestant groups. The U.S. Conference of Catholic Bishops has been proactive as

---

6. William O'Neill, "'No Longer Strangers' (Ephesians 2:19): The Ethics of Migration," *Word and World* 29, no. 3 (Summer 2009): 230.

7. From the wide range available, see Keifert, *Welcoming the Stranger,* cited above, one of the earlier and rich works on Christian hospitality and its meaning for congregational life; Matthew Soerens and Jenny Hwang, *Welcoming the Stranger: Justice, Compassion, and Truth in the Immigration Debate* (Downers Grove, Ill.: IVP, 2009); M. Daniel Carroll R., *Christians at the Border* (Grand Rapids: Baker Academic, 2008); Ched Myers and Matthew Colwell, *Our God Is Undocumented* (Maryknoll, N.Y.: Orbis, 2012); and Daniel G. Groody and Gioacchino Campese, eds., *A Promised Land, a Perilous Journey: Theological Perspectives on Migration* (Notre Dame, Ind.: University of Notre Dame Press, 2008).

well, and for good practical reason. Rising deportations of unauthorized residents often inflict wounds on the religious vitality and growth of their parishes.

There's little question that the gulf between the clear biblical imperatives to welcome the stranger and the realities of policy and practice regarding immigration constitutes one of the major ways today in which faithful discipleship should result in confrontation with civil authorities. During the first term of the Obama administration, deportations of undocumented residents proceeded at rates 50 percent higher than under the Bush administration. While the president maintained that the administration's goal was to focus on those with criminal records, of the nearly 400,000 deported in 2011, only 188,000 had prior criminal convictions.[8] These policies have had devastating impacts on families and children.

Therefore, there is a long spiritual and practical distance from the Trinitarian love so marvelously depicted in Rublev's icon, manifesting the hospitality of God both given and received, and the realities facing immigrants, both legal and unauthorized. That is the challenge, indeed a test of faithfulness, facing congregations in the United States. And it is in the concrete life of congregations where these issues must be engaged. In Christine Challiot's reflection on the Rublev icon, she quotes Father Andre Borrely, an Orthodox priest from Marseilles, France, on how the reality of this Trinitarian love is to infuse and mold the life of the congregation:

> The parish must be the place in which, patiently and ascetically, we learn to move from division to unity, from egotism to sharing, from hatred to love, from vengeance to forgiveness, from injustice to justice, from violence to peace and from death to life. It is a sphere of existence in which a man [*sic*] succeeds in unifying his personal being, where prayer and action, adoration and efficiency, contemplation and participation in history, cease to be incompatible . . . the parish is a place of re-birth. . . . In the middle of a large city, it is a place where I am offered the possibility of rooting myself in a reality that transcends this fallen world . . . (making possible) the acceptance of the

---

8. Jeremy B. White, "Under Obama, Deportations Reach Near Record Number in 2011," *International Business Times*, September 10, 2012: http://www.ibtimes.com/under-obama-deportations-near-record-number-2011-781511.

other in his or her otherness that relativizes me, the hospitable welcome of the stranger, a disinterested communion with beings and
things, a sense of festivity and of unconfined joy in celebration . . .
celebration that is a call to a "liturgy after the Liturgy" that unfolds
within the concrete and tormented history of mankind.[9]

Congregations are faced with a calling to welcome the stranger, first
of all, within the society and local community. This means ministering
to the stranger's concrete physical needs, even as Abraham and Sarah
did immediately to the three strangers outside their tent. Teaching English, finding housing, securing employment, negotiating the maze of
procedures necessary for a sustainable life in a strange new land — all
are the concrete tasks required, and hundreds of congregations are re-
sponding with "refugee task forces" to meet such needs. Beneath this is
the commitment to support refugees' dignity and protect their security
and safety in a society still filled with fear, racism, and animosity toward
the strangers in its midst, often exploited by crass politicians.

Beyond this, however, is a more ecclesiologically and practically
perplexing challenge: How does a congregation relate to, welcome, and
extend its *koinonia* to those immigrants who are practicing Christians,
or who are converted to Christianity in the midst of their sojourn? How
does our belonging to one body find concrete expression in this most
specific and vital part of the church — the local congregation? Recalling
that the vast majority of immigrants coming to the United States are
Christian, and more become Christian, this is an existential challenge
directly affecting thousands of the estimated 350,000 congregations in
the United States.[10]

A Nonassimilation Policy

My wife Karin and I are members of the Church of the Servant in Grand
Rapids, Michigan. The congregation of nearly 1,000 is comprised of
well-educated, largely white members, including many from the Calvin

9. Challiot, "Contemplating Rublev's Icon," p. 142.

10. There's no completely reliable calculation of the number of congregations in the
United States, but this figure comes from the Hartford Institute for Religion Research,
which has pioneered outstanding studies of congregational life in the United States.
http://hirr.hartsem.edu/research/fastfacts/fast_facts.html#numcong.

College and Seminary community, located nearby. The worship services are rich in liturgy, with communion celebrated every Sunday, which is extremely rare for congregations of the Reformed tradition. The arts are regarded as a rich gift of God, and are reflected in the texture of the church's worship and liturgical dance, as well as the architecture of its sanctuary. Sermons by its senior pastor, Jack Roeda, are intellectually challenging, biblically grounded, and spiritually powerful.

The congregation, like many in its parent denomination, the Christian Reformed Church of North America, has a strong education and faith formation program, with theologically stimulating classes for all ages. Further, Church of the Servant has a history of strong social outreach and ministry. In recent years that has focused particularly on teaching English as a second language (ESL) to refugees and newly arrived immigrants in the Grand Rapids area. These ESL classes brought many congregation members into close connection with these newly arrived strangers. Further, following the national pattern, many of these immigrants were Christians, or became interested in exploring Christian faith, sometimes directly because of the hospitality extended by the congregation.

Simply inviting these new, foreign-born residents to the Church of the Servant's worship service, however, had limitations. With many just struggling to master the English language, a service with a worship folder fifteen pages long, filled with complex words and expressions, and preaching geared to those used to the intellectual environment of a college, seemed inaccessible. Further, those who came with Christian experience in their homelands were almost always accustomed to worship that was far more free flowing, spiritually exuberant, and emotionally expressive.

So the church decided to start a "Basic English Service," also meeting Sunday mornings, but designed especially for these new residents. The style is far simpler, with words on screens rather than on paper, sermons sensitive to the level of English of those worshiping, and songs and prayers somewhat less scripted. The service got off the ground and gathered a small but appreciative and growing group of worshipers.

But then some in the main congregation, and the senior pastor, began to feel that the church could be in danger of "ghettoizing" these newcomers. Pragmatically the arrangement made sense, but theologically and spiritually, something seemed disjointed. The intention was to be "one body," but it felt in many ways that we were two. One summer, a lunch after the two services was instituted to bring folks together for table fellowship. It seemed to help, although many simply sat at tables with those whom they already knew.

So Church of the Servant continues its journey, begun by simple faithfulness to "welcome the stranger," but now confronted with the challenge of discerning what that means for the shape of its own life. Hospitality, it turns out, changes both the one who offers it and the one who receives it. And the tables, in unexpected ways, get turned.

The story of the congregation where my wife and I find ourselves encountering the body of Christ, in flesh and blood, is being repeated in growing numbers of congregations throughout North America — and, of course, beyond. Crucial questions come into play. How do we deal with deep cultural and social differences in the life of a local church? Isn't there a legitimate place for people to worship with those who are similar to them in tastes, education, theological outlook, and cultural background? Isn't that even a model for starting and growing new churches?

Further, what is the overall goal for those who are new immigrants in our midst? Isn't the United States the great "melting pot"? Just as with Dutch, Norwegian, German, and Italian immigrants a century ago, isn't the point to get new residents assimilated to our culture and way of life? Shouldn't the church play a role in that process?

Of course, these questions have been hotly debated in both theological and sociological circles. They come against the backdrop of the forces of globalization, the growing multiculturalism in society, and the persistent search for identity and community, felt especially keenly by new immigrants. While we will return to these broader questions, first it's worth asking how the church dealt with these issues when it was being established.

These issues were central to the early church as it was being formed. It took root within an empire exercising its own version of "globalization" in the ancient world. Multiple cultures and languages defined the context of where Jesus lived, died, and was resurrected. Even the Jerusalem church exhibited a degree of cultural diversity.[11] But when the gospel made that initial journey from Jerusalem to Antioch, following the vi-

11. From a huge range of biblical scholarship now available around these issues, I am particularly indebted to this article by Dr. Thorsten Prill, of the University of Nottingham in England, for putting these questions in the framework of immigration:

sion given to Peter and his journey to Cornelius's home, the nature of the church as a multicultural body of people became intrinsic to its understanding of God's grace, power, and reconciling love.

The leadership of the early Pauline churches, as recorded by Luke, exhibited a consistent multicultural nature. Moreover, when the Council of Jerusalem met to resolve the major conflict around the understanding of gospel and culture, at one level its answer was clear. Greeks did not have to become Jewish to be part of the community of faith. But at a deeper level, this response constituted a "nonassimilation" policy of the early church.[12] In other words, non-Jews were not required to become assimilated into Jewish culture in order to become Christian.

At the same time, reasonable adjustments were made, and agreed to mutually, to reflect the shared sensitivity of each toward the culture of the other. Further, there's no indication that a congregation should be established just for Greeks, or for Jews, within the early emerging church. The division between Greek and Jew, as well as the other primary divisions in that society between slave and free, and male and female, have all been overcome and reconciled through the power of the resurrection of Jesus Christ. They are now joined together in community, but they come as equals, in true mutuality. One group is not "assimilated" by the other.

As Korean theologian Chun-Hoi Heo writes in *Multicultural Christology:* "The price of peace is not the elimination of differences. Jews and gentiles worship together in Christ while both remain Jews and gentiles. Jesus and his followers do not aim to create a generic community of cultural homogeneity, but rather to reconcile them to God and to one another by respecting both ethnic groups as mutually interdependent. We are entrusted with that ministry of reconciliation."[13]

Can All Tribes Be Gathered?

The picture of the New Testament church as a reconciled and reconciling community is compelling and clear. And it is in stark contrast to the reality of most congregations in the United States. As author Soong-Chan

"Migration, Mission, and the Multi-ethnic Church," *Evangelical Review of Theology* 33, no. 4 (2009): 332-46.

12. Prill, "Migration, Mission, and the Multi-ethnic Church," p. 344.

13. Chun-Hoi Heo, *Multicultural Christology: A Korean Immigrant Perspective* (Bern: Peter Lang, 2005), p. 205.

Rah points out, "less than 6% of American churches are multiethnic."[14] This uses a generous definition of at least 20 percent of the congregation being from one racial-ethnic background, and 80 percent from another.

The vast majority of congregations in the United States begin from a homogeneous starting point that regards the New Testament vision of a reconciled, multiracial community as a distant, unrealistic dream. But the ongoing patterns of migration to the United States, with the growing racial and ethnic diversity in our society, threaten to turn the present reality of U.S. congregations into an ethical and theological nightmare. How long can children attend schools where twenty-five different languages are present, and then go to churches where there is one, or maybe two, without eventually concluding that the words and stories they hear don't seem true to what they experience?

Yet, building a true multiracial congregation is a task so difficult that it makes the reconciling power of the gospel indispensable. A decade ago, four authors from diverse racial backgrounds collaborated in writing *United by Faith,* a book that set forth the theological rationale and a compelling case for building multiracial congregations.[15] While many other works had addressed these questions (the book's bibliography cites over 200 books and articles), *United by Faith* had a strong impact in both evangelical and mainline Protestant circles. It wasn't just a study, but a call to create multiracial congregations as a faithful expression of the gospel and a response to the sin of racism.

Stories of multiracial congregations with powerful ministries, including those started years earlier, are inspiring and demonstrate what's possible. In Little Rock, Arkansas, Pastor Mark DeYmaz began feeling uncomfortable that "the only minorities in my otherwise wonderful, healthy church were janitors."[16] In 2001, he made a commitment to plant a multiethnic church called Mosaic. Today it's a thriving ministry with campuses in Conway, Arkansas, and Durham, North

14. "Harder Than Anyone Can Imagine" (interview with four pastors, including Soong-Chan Rah), *Christianity Today,* April 2005, p. 37. Findings from the National Congregations Study funded by the Lilly Endowment and directed by Mark Chaves puts this figure at 7 percent.

15. Curtiss Paul DeYoung, Michael O. Emerson, George Yancey, and Karen Chai Kim, *United by Faith: The Multiracial Congregation as an Answer to the Problem of Race* (Oxford and New York: Oxford University Press, 2003).

16. "Diverse by Design" (interview with Mark DeYmaz), *Leadership* 9, no. 3 (Summer 2008): 15.

Carolina, as well as in Little Rock, and a staff reflecting the multiracial vision of the congregation.

Strongly evangelical in doctrine and teaching, DeYmaz has also been instrumental in starting a network for other multiethnic churches called the Mosaix Global Network. Its goal is to see 20 percent of congregations in the United States achieve 20 percent racial diversity in their membership by the year 2020. DeYmaz says simply, "If your church is not diverse in the next 15-20 years in America, it's going to be largely irrelevant. In an increasingly diverse and cynical society, people are no longer going to buy into the message that God loves all people when it's preached from segregated pulpits and pews."[17]

Erwin McManus is probably better known as the leader of Mosaic church in Los Angeles. McManus, who grew up in El Salvador, moved the congregation, originally a white Baptist church, in radically new directions. With a postmodern flavor and high-tech style, the mostly younger congregation of around 3,000 gathers at seven different campuses in the Los Angeles area, and is highly diverse racially. McManus is a popular speaker, particularly in the evangelical world.

Pentecostals will point to the multiracial nature of those who experienced the outpouring of the Holy Spirit at Azusa Street, Los Angeles, in 1906, led by William Seymour, an African American preacher. Today, the largest church in the Vineyard association of congregations is in Columbus, Ohio, and its pastor, Rich Nathan, has pressed to see that it reflects the racial diversity of its city. Presently immigrants and refugees from 104 nations are part of the congregation, and 28 percent of the 9,000 who attend are from racial backgrounds other than the majority Anglo ethnic group in Columbus.[18]

These three examples of significantly multiracial megachurches are all evangelical or Pentecostal, which should not be surprising. While mainline Protestants have long championed in courageous ways the call to racial reconciliation, many congregations in urban areas that reflect a deep multiethnic character are from more evangelical or Pentecostal traditions. Some research has shown that there are fewer mainline Protestant congregations that are genuinely multiracial. However, Michael Emerson, author of *People of the Dream: Multiracial Congrega-*

17. "Diverse by Design," p. 15.

18. Katelyn Beaty, "The Kingdom in Columbus," *Christianity Today,* December 2011, pp. 42-45.

tions in the United States, whose work was based on six years of data collection and research, found that conservative versus liberal theology was not a factor in the emergence of multiracial congregations. What did make a difference was a more charismatic worship style, which often correlated with greater racial diversity.[19]

Examples and stories of multiracial congregations in mainline Protestantism give hope to those from this tradition, even if they may not seem as frequent. In my own denomination, the Reformed Church in America, Rev. Jacqui Lewis has played a pioneering role in leading Middle Collegiate Church, in the East Village in lower Manhattan, to be a thriving multiracial congregation. Rev. Lewis also builds networks with other congregations across the United States seeking a similar vision. Hundreds are on that journey.

Catholic parishes, of course, are far more likely to have racial diversity in their members, given the patterns of immigration to the United States. But in those cases, the challenge is whether different racial and ethnic groups that are present in a Catholic parish can build a life of rich interrelationships, or whether they will remain clustered in their respective homogeneous units.

What's clear across the theological spectrum is that building congregations with an authentic multiracial life is hard work. Mark Chaves, who led the National Congregations Study, supported by the Lilly Endowment, wrote this in his recent book summarizing key trends in American religion:

> Sociologists and others have paid a lot of attention recently to what we might call *deeply* diverse congregations, meaning congregations that have, say, equal numbers of blacks and whites, or that have a relatively equal mix of blacks, whites, and Asians, or in which there is a sizeable proportion of Latinos among predominantly white non-Hispanics. But this sort of truly multiethnic or multicultural congregation — congregations with more than a smattering of minority presence — remains very rare and difficult to sustain over the long run. And there is no increase in recent years in this sort of congregation.[20]

19. Michael O. Emerson with Rodney M. Woo, *People of the Dream: Multiracial Congregations in the United States* (Princeton: Princeton University Press, 2006), p. 50.

20. Mark Chaves, *American Religion: Contemporary Trends* (Princeton: Princeton University Press, 2011), p. 28.

But Chaves does find signs of change encouraging to anyone believing that the local congregation should be a foretaste of God's desire for those of every tongue and tribe to worship together as one united community. The number of predominantly white congregations that now have some presence of African Americans, Latinos, or Asian Americans is steadily increasing. Specifically, for congregations that are at least 90 percent white, some African Americans are present in 36 percent of them; Latinos are present in 32 percent; and Asians in 20 percent.[21] Those congregations don't yet meet the goal of what is expected for a genuinely multiracial congregation. But they do demonstrate this simple fact: the number of "white only" congregations in the United States is steadily decreasing, and this trend will accelerate.

What matters particularly for the focus of this book is whether local congregations in the global North, experiencing through patterns of immigration the presence of the global church in their midst, can become places that discover unity in the face of the divisions within world Christianity. The task of building multiracial congregations is painfully difficult in part because the rifts in the body of Christ are so pervasive and deep, and because the sin of racism is so strong. Persevering in that task is not only a response of simple faithfulness to the gospel, but also, in our time, a critical form of participation in our common ecumenical journey.

Practices to Share

1. Mission Comes First

Those who are building multiracial congregations, and those who study them, seem to agree that becoming multiracial isn't the goal in and of itself. Rather, becoming multiracial results from a deep, internalized sense of the congregation's mission. For instance, it may also be the fruit of a commitment to evangelistic outreach, or to expressing concrete acts of justice and solidarity in the community. The stark and indicting reality, confirmed by the research of Michael Emerson and his colleagues, is that in the United States, "the vast majority of congregations are substantially less racially diverse than the neighborhoods in which they reside."[22] A multiracial congregation is one of those rare

21. Chaves, *American Religion*, p. 29.
22. Emerson, *People of the Dream*, p. 44.

and powerful exceptions that, at times, becomes even more racially diverse than its neighborhood. Often, a missional attentiveness and commitment to the world right outside its doors is a first step leading a congregation on a path toward becoming more multiracial.

2. Intentionality Is Essential

The desire for a multiracial future has to be genuinely owned by the congregation. Moreover, this needs to be embraced not as a strategy, or a means of survival, but as a biblically rooted commitment to justice and equity. Whether through means of a mission statement, consistent teaching, discernment of vision, or the calling of pastoral leadership, welcoming the gift of a multiracial future needs to become deeply and intentionally grafted into the hopes, dreams, and prayers of the congregation.

3. Diversity in Leadership

No one can doubt that multiracial leadership is essential to a multiracial congregation. Developing that leadership early, and intentionally, is essential. Again, this isn't merely good strategy. Thorsten Prill argues that it reflects what was happening in Luke's account of the New Testament churches in Antioch, Philippi, Thessalonica, Beroea, and Corinth: "It is significant that the leadership of these churches reflected not only the diverse local church membership but also the diversity of the whole body of Christ. . . . It follows that it is mandatory for multi-ethnic churches to select their leaders on this basis and to avoid mono-ethnic leadership."[23]

4. Mixed Ministry Teams

Not only the leadership, but also the various teams, task forces, and mission groups that make up a congregation's life need to reflect the multiethnic diversity that is being desired. This becomes particularly

23. Prill, "Migration, Mission, and the Multi-ethnic Church," p. 345.

important in building a congregational life with new immigrants. The posture of established members serving new immigrants, while initially a natural expression of mercy and compassion, has to be transformed into mutuality, allowing for those opportunities for God's mysterious presence to turn the tables of hospitality.

5. Ongoing Christian Formation

As the congregation grows on its journey, its mission, vision, and values require continual reinforcement through its efforts in the forming of disciples. The biblical practice of hospitality, and its radical meaning within both the Hebrew Scriptures and the life and ministry of Jesus, needs to be absorbed by the hearts and minds of congregants. Likewise, addressing the sin of racism and utilizing the tools of antiracism training in an ongoing way are part of an overall process of Christian formation for a multiracial community of believers.

6. Prepare for a Long Journey

Building a multiracial church is a slow, careful, and often painstaking process. People in a congregation are at different points in their own journey to embrace a multiracial community. Pastoral patience is required as they move through steps in this process. Further, for the congregation as a whole, this pilgrimage moves through stages. That's particularly true for an existing congregation that makes a commitment to a multiracial future, in contrast to a multiracial new church plant. But for all, this is an arduous journey requiring discernment, perseverance, time, and trust in the working of God's Spirit.

These six qualities, in my judgment, are essential in the spiritual quest of any who feel called by God to participate in the building and shaping of a multiracial congregation as a visible witness to the prayer of Jesus that we all may be one.

Of course, some practitioners who have been leading the development of multiracial congregations offer various versions of the steps and qualities they have discovered as crucial, and these reflect generally the qualities that I've summarized above. Mark DeYmaz, for instance, in *Building a Healthy Multi-ethnic Church,* identifies a set of seven commitments that are needed, namely: "Embrace Dependence (upon God)," "Take Intentional Steps," "Empower Diverse Leadership," "Develop Cross-Cultural Relationships," "Pursue Cross-Cultural Competence," "Promote a Spirit of Inclusion," and "Mobilize for Impact." The book draws on the wisdom of others in exploring how these relate to planting a new multiethnic church, revitalizing a congregation in decline, and transforming an existing homogeneous church.[24]

An example from the mainline Protestant tradition is found in Stephanie Spellers's book *Radical Welcome*. She stresses in helpful ways how a congregation needs to move beyond simply "welcome" and "inclusion" to reimaging its common life.[25] An Episcopal priest who pastors the Crossing, an emergent worshiping congregation hosted by St. Paul's Cathedral in Boston, Rev. Spellers preached at the Episcopal Convention in July 2012, and said this:

> Here's what our legendary welcome sounds like: "The Episcopal Church Welcomes You. We're so glad you're here! Now, this is the Book of Common Prayer. Obey it. This is our musical tradition. Master it. This is our English heritage. Adopt it. This is our sense of order. Assimilate it. And the gifts from your home culture, your young culture, your lower-class culture? Would you leave them at the door and pick them up on your way out? They're not quite Episcopal enough."[26]

Starting a new multiracial congregation, while a tremendously challenging task, offers one the advantage of being able to establish the congregation's unique DNA from its inception. Often that makes it easier to navigate the journey, compared to transforming existing congregations. Take the Bridgeway Community Church begun in Columbia,

24. Mark DeYmaz, *Building a Healthy Multi-ethnic Church: Mandate, Commitments, and Practices of a Diverse Congregation* (San Francisco: Jossey-Bass/John Wiley, 2007). The chapter on revitalizing a declining congregation into a multiracial one is written by Rodney Woo, based on his experience with Wilcrest Baptist Church in Houston. Woo also assisted Michael Emerson in the writing of *People of the Dream,* cited above, which studied Wilcrest Baptist Church extensively as one of its models.

25. Stephanie Spellers, *Radical Welcome: Embracing God, the Other, and the Spirit of Transformation* (New York: Church Publishing, 2006).

26. "Stephanie Spellers Preaches at Convention Eucharist," Episcopal News Service, July 11, 2012: http://episcopaldigitalnetwork.com/ens/2012/07/11/the-rev-stephanie-spellers-preaches-at-convention-eucharist/.

Maryland, by an interracial core group of six people in 1992, including David Anderson, its founding pastor. With roots in the evangelical tradition, they shared a vision "to be a multicultural body of fully-devoted followers of Christ moving forward in unity and love to reach our community, our culture and our world for Jesus Christ."[27]

Today Bridgeway is a congregation of about 3,000, comprised of roughly half who are black (mostly African American but some African), a quarter white, and others Hispanic and Asian.[28] The Sunday I visited, a high-octane band led contemporary worship, and worship leaders wore T-shirts with the word "Gracist" on the front. Anderson's preaching connected deeply with the congregation. He's also the author of *Multicultural Ministry: Finding Your Church's Unique Rhythm.*[29]

Yet, starting new multiracial congregations cannot be the only pathway for gathering "all tribes and peoples . . . before the throne" (Revelation 7:9). Even as existing congregations are becoming more multiracial by default through demographic change in society, they will not make the transition and flourish as a genuinely multiracial congregation without clear intentionality, and a focused mission, which then becomes the catalyst for the transformation of its congregational culture.

In *United by Faith,* the research done by its authors prompted them to delineate three models of multiracial congregations. First is the "assimilated" type. Here, one race remains dominant, and it's expected that the minority race or races, even if more than 20 percent of the total, will simply be assimilated into the prevailing culture. It's what often happens, even subconsciously, in well-intentioned congregations that haven't absorbed the "nonassimilation policy" of the book of Acts.

Next is the "pluralist" multiracial congregation. Here, elements of the different cultures present in the congregation are incorporated into worship and church activities, and members have a growing sense of ownership. Yet, social interaction between those of different races doesn't generally take place outside the church. It's a step forward on the journey, but more of a negotiated reflection of diversity rather than a deeper and fuller integration.

Third is the "integrated" multiracial congregation. By this the au-

---

27. The vision statement is taken from the Bridgeway Community Church website: http://bridgewayonline.org/about/mission-vision-values/.

28. Emerson, *People of the Dream,* p. 167.

29. David A. Anderson, *Multicultural Ministry: Finding Your Church's Unique Rhythm* (Grand Rapids: Zondervan, 2004).

thors mean that instead of simply making accommodations to the variety of cultural and racial expressions, the whole congregational culture is transformed. A new "hybrid" culture emerges reflecting the unity in diversity being created by God's Spirit. No group is dominant, and an equality and a mutuality exist among all those of different races. The practical distinctions between "us" and "them" recede in the midst of the new culture that is being created.[30]

Of course, this last model is the ideal. But the authors stress, correctly, that fundamental issues of structure and power must be addressed in order to achieve a genuine transformation of congregational culture. And such a transformation is essential for becoming a multiracial congregation that can thrive as a living microcosm of the unity given in the body of Christ. The authors express it this way: "In our opinion, a truly effective multiracial congregation not only reflects aspects of the cultures represented by congregation members, but it reflects a new and unique culture that transcends the worldly cultures. Such churches create a new mestizaje congregational culture by relying on the distinctiveness of its different cultures and peoples to create a unity far more complete than can be done otherwise."[31]

Seeking such a transformation in congregational culture is imperative. The power of race runs deep, and is embedded in prevailing structures and unconscious assumptions. Particularly given the tormented history of relationships between blacks and whites in the United States, serious barriers confront the genuine mutuality essential to becoming an authentic multiracial congregation.

Sociologist Korie L. Edwards studied this deeply in her book *The Elusive Dream*.[32] Taking the case study of a Midwestern congregation with a mix of African Americans, who were in the majority, and white members, she studied intently its structure, patterns of power, and decision making. Her conclusion was that in the end, the congregation functioned through the power of ingrained preferences and practices of its white members. This led her to conclude that interracial congregations "work to the extent that they are, first, comfortable places for whites to attend."[33]

30. DeYoung et al., *United by Faith*, pp. 164-69.

31. DeYoung et al., *United by Faith*, p. 169.

32. Korie L. Edwards, *The Elusive Dream: The Power of Race in Interracial Churches* (Oxford: Oxford University Press, 2008).

33. Edwards, *The Elusive Dream*, p. 6.

Proving Edwards's assumption wrong comes only through embracing the mutuality and equality found at the core of the New Testament church's vision and experience. Edwards concludes her work with this challenge:

> As churches seek to become more interracial, they must not be satisfied with simply having people of different racial groups worship together. They must not even be satisfied with people fellowshipping from time to time outside of church activities. If churches want to realize Dr. King's dream, they must first embrace a dream of racial justice and equality. Interracial churches must be places that all racial groups can call their own, where all racial groups have the power to influence the minor and major decisions of the church, where the culture and experiences of all racial groups are not just tolerated, but appreciated. This demands a radical approach and is certainly a high calling.[34]

As we reflect on the presence of 43 million residents in the United States born in another country, and ponder the trends that will increase the flow of new strangers and aliens in our land, as well as the growth of those presently here, it becomes clear that our society is being fundamentally transformed. In coming years there will be no racial majority in the United States. In many locations, that describes the present reality.

So the question becomes clear. Will congregations in the United States be capable of the transformation that is essential for them to be signs of the hospitality, justice, mutuality, and reconciliation that reflect God's intention and love? Moreover, will congregations become the local laboratories of ecclesiology that demonstrate how the entrenched divisions in world Christianity can find expressions of that unity, which is both a gift and an obligation?

We're taken back to Andrei Rublev's icon of the Trinity. The Russian Orthodox Archpriest Vladimir Borozdinov reflected theologically on this icon in an article some years ago. Explaining how the nature and functioning of the Trinity are portrayed in the icon, he said this: "Every Person of the Holy Trinity, living by their mutual Holy Love, strives towards their unity and perfect proximity, trying to be as close as possible

---

34. Edwards, *The Elusive Dream*, p. 140.

One to the Other and devote Oneself to the Other as fully as possible, offering the Other complete freedom of action in Himself."[35]

This is a moving description of how the Trinitarian love of God flows between each person in full mutuality, responsiveness, interdependence, and equality. That's the nature of God's love, and it is this love that has been poured into our hearts through the Holy Spirit (Romans 5:5). Moreover, this is the love that forms the foundation for the life of the body of Christ, the church.

This same love flows not only between the persons of the Trinity, and not only among those called to the body, but it also reaches out in generous hospitality to the world. The circle is open in the icon, even as the circle is to be open when that love fills the body of Christ. The profound mutuality and equality necessary at the foundation of a multiracial congregation are derived from the Trinitarian love of God. The qualities describing how the persons of the Trinity are interacting with one another in Rublev's icon provide the inspiring description of how those brought into the circle of the Trinitarian love are to respond to one another in a worshiping community filled with the gifts of God-given diversity.

Welcoming the stranger into the life and love of a congregation, an action so indispensable for discovering anew the unity of the body, is nothing more, or less, than participating in the love of the Trinity.

35. Archpriest Vladimir Borozdinov, "'The Holy Trinity' of Andrei Rublev," *Journal of the Moscow Patriarchate* 7 (1990): 75.

CHAPTER TEN

Under the Ecclesiological Radar

Joel Carpenter, director of the Nagel Institute at Calvin College, taught an adult education class at our church in Grand Rapids, Michigan, on the changes in world Christianity. As a "homework assignment," he asked us to use the Yellow Pages, Google, or any other means to find out how many immigrant congregations were in the Grand Rapids area. By this, he meant congregations formed by Christians who had migrated to the area recently, in the past couple of decades.

Joel did the same assignment. The results revealed eleven Latino congregations, and these were in addition to the increase in Hispanic parishioners in the area's Catholic churches. Two Ethiopian congregations were found, one of them independent evangelical and the other Ethiopian Orthodox, worshiping at the St. Nicolas Antiochian Orthodox Church just a few blocks from the church where our class was meeting. Three Korean congregations were easily located since two of them were affiliated with the Christian Reformed Church.

Nearby in Holland, Michigan, there are both a Laotian and a Cambodian church. Not far from my home, a Vietnamese congregation worships. Grand Rapids has at least one Chinese Christian Church, and a pan-African congregation with a Nigerian and a Kenyan as copastors. Further, there are two Sudanese congregations — one CRC and one Anglican. This list is by no means comprehensive, since no agency or group really keeps track of these immigrant congregations. But it's an indication of the presence of immigrant congregations from the global South in a Midwestern city of under 200,000, and known generally for its Dutch heritage and as the home of former Republican President Gerald Ford.

Such congregations are generally not on our church-finders' radar unless our local church is renting its facility to one of these groups on Sundays after its regular, predominantly white services have concluded. Yet, such congregations are growing everywhere, and particularly in large urban centers. Mark Gornik in *Word Made Global* estimates that New York City is host to at least 150 African immigrant congregations,[1] and they reflect the diversity of Christianity within the world's most Christian continent. Hundreds more immigrant congregations thrive and grow within the radius of this world city.

This picture continues, however, throughout the land. Minneapolis–St. Paul, for instance, long known for its Scandinavian and German heritage, has seen an influx of immigrants from Africa, Asia, and Latin America. A decade ago, Frieder Ludwig, then a faculty member at Luther Seminary, became attentive to the presence of immigrant congregations in the area. Joining with others, including Dana K. Nelson, a student, he discovered sixty-seven congregations of Asian immigrants and seventy-three congregations of African immigrants in the Twin Cities.[2] (Their search was limited to African and Asian immigrant congregations.) Fifty-two of these congregations, one for each Sunday, were profiled in a small but revealing book, *Mission and Migration.*

The diversity in the types of those congregations gives a picture of how immigrant local churches in general are established. Some were nondenominational; several were affiliated with African-based denominations; in many other cases they were part of the Lutheran church (ELCA) or other U.S. denominations; and three were Orthodox (Ethiopian Orthodox and Coptic Orthodox).

The reasons immigrants chose either to join a mono-ethnic congregation comprised primarily of other immigrants from their same culture and faith tradition, or a multiracial congregation in which they are one among other racial and ethnic groups, are complex. Some sociologists of religion who have studied these questions have devised six "types" of immigrant congregations, from mono-ethnic congregations that tightly maintain their homogeneity to multiethnic congregations with several immigrant groups, and other forms in between those two.[3]

1. Mark R. Gornik, *Word Made Global: Stories of African Christianity in New York City* (Grand Rapids: Eerdmans, 2011), p. 4.

2. Dana K. Nelson, *Mission and Migration: Fifty-two African and Asian Congregations in Minnesota* (Minneapolis: Lutheran University Press, 2007), pp. 10-11.

3. Helen Rose Fuchs Ebaugh and Janet Saltzman Chafetz, *Religion and the New Immi-*

Immigrants may navigate their way among these various congregations during the course of their pilgrimage in a new land for a variety of reasons.

Beyond various sociological factors, however, is the underlying presence of genuine hospitality, or its absence. Harvey Kwiyani, a doctoral student from Malawi at Luther Seminary, wrote his dissertation centering on the question of hospitality toward African immigrant Christians, and used three congregations in the Twin Cities as case studies.[4] All three he examined had a presence of African immigrants.

First was a congregation of the Evangelical Lutheran Church in America known for its multiracial composition. Second was a Lutheran congregation (not ELCA) that was charismatic. Third was a large independent, Pentecostal church. Kwiyani's research involved carefully constructed ethnographic methods to discover the actual experience of African immigrants in each of these congregations.

The results were revealing. Despite the good intentions and desires of the ELCA congregation, the African immigrant members sensed that its hospitality never went beyond the social level. A sense of "us" and "them" remained. A similar situation was experienced at the other Lutheran church, which was charismatic. As Kwiyani describes, "As the immigrants seemed to be on the receiving end of all hospitality at all times, it was hard for the participants to imagine the Spirit moving through an immigrant to minister to the locals."[5]

The Pentecostal congregation, however, had made a commitment to see itself as a "house of prayer for all nations." Gifts of those from all racial groups were welcomed, and people were encouraged to grow into their leadership potential. Again, to quote Kwiyani: "At the center of their identity is the conviction that the Spirit is at work in the congregation and that it can use anybody, local or foreign, to get the work done. This has led to a more dynamic and confident African participation in

---

grants: *Continuities and Adaptations in Immigrant Congregations* (Walnut Creek, Calif.: AltaMira, 2000).

4. Harvey Kwiyani, "Pneumatology, Mission, and African Christians in Multicultural Congregations in North America: The Case of Three Congregations in Minneapolis and Saint Paul, Minnesota, USA" (Ph.D. diss., Luther Seminary, 2011). Kwiyani's whole dissertation is a masterful presentation of the overall question of African immigrant Christians in the United States, and the theological challenges and missiological opportunities created by their presence.

5. Kwiyani, "Pneumatology, Mission, and African Christians," p. 133.

the congregation than that which was witnessed at the other two congregations. [Its] understanding of the Spirit has made it possible for Africans to belong."[6] Kwiyani's research of these three congregations, which he placed within the overall history and framework of African migration, "reverse mission," and the understanding of the Holy Spirit, describes the realities facing a wide range of immigrant Christians in the United States. Clearly, one underlying factor determining whether they will find themselves spiritually energized and nurtured in a multiracial congregation, or whether they will enthusiastically participate in a mono-ethnic congregation of fellow immigrant Christians, is the quality of hospitality they encounter.

Of course, other factors play a strong role as well. Many good reasons draw immigrant Christians to mono-ethnic congregations when they arrive in this new land. And in fact, this is how most Christians living in the United States who were born in another country find their congregational homes. There is no question that such congregations provide a sense of security, identity, and a living reminder of their home culture. But some sociologists simply stop there, assuming that as younger generations become assimilated into the larger secular culture, these immigrant congregations will slowly die out.

But that's not the whole story. More is going on. First of all, the faith of Christian immigrants — and that of other religious immigrants, for that matter — usually becomes stronger and more intense through their whole experience. Stephen Warner, a discerning sociologist who has probed deeply the significance of the religious lives of immigrants and their congregations, puts it this way: "Immigrants [do not] . . . merely cling to what they had before they left their home countries. As religion becomes less taken for granted under the pluralistic and more secular conditions prevailing in the United States, adherents become more conscious of their tradition and often more determined about its transmission. Religion identities nominally assigned at birth become objects of active persuasion."[7]

Second, mono-ethnic immigrant congregations become the places where the practices and understandings of faith find means for adapt-

6. Kwiyani, "Pneumatology, Mission, and African Christians," p. 133.

7. R. Stephen Warner and Judith G. Wittner, eds., *Gatherings in Diaspora: Religious Communities and the New Immigration* (Philadelphia: Temple University Press, 1998), p. 17.

ing to the new cultural context in America while maintaining the core of Christian identity formed in one's culture of origin. In other words, such congregations can remind immigrants that they do not need to become wholly assimilated into Western, American culture, and that their own Christian identity, forged in their homeland, can guard them against the spiritual dangers encountered in the secular culture of their new land. At the same time, their faith can find appropriate ways of adapting to its new setting. This is not unlike the story of Acts 15, when Greeks did not have to adopt Jewish culture to be followers of Christ, but were willing to make reasonable changes in some of their practices.

Third, mono-ethnic immigrant congregations in the United States have important influences on practices, livelihood, and ministry of churches in their homeland. Increasingly, the flows of people, ideas, money, and media go back and forth within a world of global connections. Nigerian pastors in Minnesota return to their homeland for evangelistic crusades. Radio broadcasts of church services in immigrant congregations in New York or Houston are followed by those in Monrovia or Accra. These two-way flows provide means for missional connections and outreach to occur in creative and mutually reinforcing ways.[8]

J. Kwabena Asamoah-Gyadu, a noted theologian and scholar from Ghana, describes perceptively the ways in which the power of Pentecostal experiences is transmitted and shared through the media: "The expansion and appropriation of modern media technologies — particularly television, radio, and the internet — have enabled the transmission of charismatic power across the borders in ways that were unthinkable a decade ago. For example, people call into the early prayer morning sessions on Accra's Joy and Peace FM stations from New York and Toronto asking for prayers as they pursue employment opportunities or wrestle with immigration problems."[9]

---

8. Some sociologists focusing on religion of immigrant communities are giving new attention to the significance of these "transnational" movements of ideas, beliefs, and practices between immigrant congregations and those in their original homeland. See, for example, Helen Rose Ebaugh, "Transnationality and Religion in Immigrant Congregations: The Global Impact," *Nordic Journal of Religion and Society* 23, no. 2 (2010): 105-19.

9. J. Kwabena Asamoah-Gyadu, "Mediating Spiritual Power: African Christianity, Transnationalism and the Media," in *Religion Crossing Boundaries: Transnational Religious and Social Dynamics in Africa and the New African Diaspora,* ed. Afeosemime U. Adogame and James V. Spickard (Leiden: Brill, 2010), p. 88.

Asamoah-Gyadu explains further the way in which books, tapes, and similar media become the means for believers to receive an "anointing" through this sharing across boundaries: "For both their producers and consumers, these media materials possess a sacramental value, in which physical things are conduits for ontological graces."[10]

Similar examples involving Hispanics and Asian Americans demonstrate how lived Christian faith in the immigrant experience is reinforced through ongoing connections between their new mono-ethnic congregations and those they left in their homeland. Such congregations play an important role in the quest of immigrants to find roots for their Christian identity in a new society where they constantly are struggling to discover, in the words of the New Testament, how to be in the world but not of the world. At the same time, these congregations face their own challenges of how to adjust their life to issues like worship style, use of English, the role of women, and transitions in leadership, especially as they relate to the next generation.

Identity in the Midst of Globalization

Beneath the issues surrounding the participation of Christian immigrants in mono-ethnic or multiracial congregations is the fundamental question: How does non-Western Christianity encounter the church within post-Christian Western culture? That is the pressing drama now being played out in the pilgrimage of world Christianity. Discovering the unity of the body of Christ in the twenty-first century will depend primarily on how churches embrace and respond to the narratives of this drama.

As we've said, today this global story is being told and encountered in local settings. It raises searching questions, such as the meaning of globalization for the life of the world church. More specifically, are we all being drawn into one globalized "melting pot" that will resolve both the interaction of cultures and the options for Christian practice? Will immigrant Christians assimilate the patterns of faith and expression long established in the West in the same way that their taste buds learn to delight in a McDonald's double cheeseburger?

Or are we seeking other options, perhaps more difficult and less

10. Asamoah-Gyadu, "Mediating Spiritual Power," p. 98.

obvious? Does the faith of immigrant Christians bring a unique witness, forged in a non-Western context, to a secularized culture dominated by a rationalist and materialist worldview? Are the questions around identity, assimilation, and globalization faced by immigrant Christians in the West pivotal to how world Christianity engages its most serious divisions?

When we speak of "globalization," a whole host of differing and complex meanings are involved. At one level, this refers to the obvious ways in which the communications revolution as well as travel have built endless means of contact and connections that bypass existing national and geographical boundaries. We function in a deeply connected global environment. Several years ago, when my son, J.K., was a teacher in a fairly remote part of China, and I was traveling in Africa, I reached him over Skype from an Internet connection at an airport, and we had a valuable conversation. That's one level of what "globalization" means.

But at another level, globalization refers to the economic process of integrating commerce and markets in ways that erode national barriers. Capital moves freely through trade as various restrictions are continually removed. Labor likewise gets allocated by global forces that transcend national, political, or social restraints. The theory is that wealth increases faster and more efficiently, and that should be to the benefit of all.

In practice, however, the forces of such economic globalization always leave some on the margins. Capital doesn't flow only to places that maximize its efficiency. It also flows away from places. Many become excluded from the promised benefits of globalization. Further, the wealth created is in the hands of corporations that become liberated from various restraints imposed by states regarding fair wages, environmental protections, safety of workers, and protection of local communities. Granted, there are huge debates over these questions, far beyond our scope for this purpose. But the simple point is that economic globalization has losers as well as winners, and leaves groups of people marginalized from its fruits.

Globalization also refers to the development of a unified, global culture, created and guided by the emergence of a single, integrated market. Some have argued that this also means that ideology of all kinds is marginalized in the "end of history." One homogeneous monoculture develops globally, linked together by shared tastes in music, entertainment, and even dining, allowing Kentucky Fried Chicken to find astonishing growth in China. A commercial, consumerist drive propelled by materialism unites people, and especially younger global generations, beyond the boundaries of local culture, political philosophy, and religious beliefs.

How does the shift in world Christianity to the global South and East, and migration from there to the global North, fit into the process of globalization, and the debate over its consequences? First, at one level, the globalization of communication and travel probably has accelerated the growth of Christianity in Asia, Africa, and Latin America. Simply put, the Word travels faster. Communication has endless possibilities for allowing the message of the gospel to be shared in ways that were barely imaginable even a couple of decades ago.

However, the effects of economic globalization strike hard. Many of those marginalized by its unjust allocation of benefits are also in regions and sectors of society where Christianity is growing the fastest. In particular, much of the growth of Pentecostal and other indigenous expressions of Christianity is among those excluded from the direct economic benefits of globalization. Thus, the shift in world Christianity provides a living prophetic critique of the promises of economic globalization.

Perhaps most important, however, is the spiritual and theological rebuke that should arise from world Christianity, now freed from the dominance of Western Christendom, to the lure of a homogeneous, materialist consumer culture offering a unified vision for life's fulfillment. Here in particular, expressions of non-Western Christianity offer a decisively alternative vision, shaped by a worldview that discerns spiritual reality saturating one's life in the world, and offering a way of life rooted first in community rather than in individualism, nurtured by self-giving love, and motivated by God's mission in the world.

These questions become deeply existential in the life of Christian immigrants and their congregations, whether multiracial or monoethnic. It is their Christian identity, shaped in non-Western settings, that assures them that their response to life in the West is not to dive into some imagined "melting pot." Rather, they can find the ways in which their faith and church community assist them in expressing an identity and witness that are true to the experience of God's Holy Spirit in their lives, and demonstrate their practical allegiance to Jesus Christ.

As Western culture becomes increasingly secular and post-Christian, the urgent need is for a genuine pluralism to develop, where voices and practices of Christians (as well as those of other faiths) that are rooted in an alternative spiritual vision from the prevailing culture are respected and engaged in public discourse, and make a contribution in shaping the common good of society. Christians whose roots of faith and life developed outside of the West, and now have migrated there, will become particularly critical to the development of such a genuine pluralism.

Once again, we're reminded of what Jehu Hanciles has written in *Beyond Christendom,* stating that every Christian migrant is a potential missionary.[11] A deeply missional engagement with Western culture, which is the goal of the missional church movement, can be animated by those who come as strangers to this land, with fresh eyes and earnest hearts. Mission and migration in the coming decades will become linked together in ever more critical ways.

The presence and witness of non-Western immigrant congregations in the midst of established churches and denominations in the United States must become a matter of spiritual and practical attention to the wider church. Building relationships between established and immigrant congregations is essential for at least two reasons. First, a climate of mutuality and ecclesiological hospitality needs to be created so a genuine theological dialogue and spiritual solidarity can begin to take root. Second, the missional witness of the church in Western culture can only take place in deeply engaging ways if the voices of non-Western Christianity are a primary part of the dialogue. Once again, this offers a pathway for building bridges across the divisions of world Christianity within our own local contexts, where the global has become local, even as the Word became flesh.

---

11. Jehu Hanciles, *Beyond Christendom: Globalization, African Migration, and the Transformation of the West* (Maryknoll, N.Y.: Orbis, 2008), p. 6. A wide range of literature addresses the impact of globalization from the viewpoint of Christian ethics. For the purposes of this chapter, I found Part I, "Transforming the Margins," of *Beyond Christendom,* pages 10-136, to be especially helpful as an integrated treatment of the subject, and I am indebted to Jehu Hanciles' work.

CHAPTER ELEVEN

"In Each Place . . . and in All Places"

New Delhi, India, was the site of the Third Assembly of the World Council of Churches, held in 1961. This was a critical juncture in the emerging life of the WCC, since nearly all the Orthodox churches officially joined and were welcomed into membership. While Orthodox voices were present in early and formative ecumenical discussions, by entering fully into WCC's life at this assembly, it became evident that this was not merely a Protestant initiative.

The assembly was featured on the cover of *Time* magazine; the cover story maintained that the "ecumenical century" was at hand. This was seen not only in the WCC gathering in New Delhi but also in the forthcoming "ecumenical council" of the Catholic Church called by Pope John XXIII, to begin in 1962 (Vatican II), and in the progress in the United States of the National Council of Churches. With journalistic ecumenical optimism, *Time* declared that "scandalous disunity among Christians [has] cheapened the church . . . the scattered forces of Christian faith are realigning and regrouping."[1]

The New Delhi Assembly adopted an important Statement on Unity as well. Shaped by its Faith and Order Commission meeting in St. Andrews, Scotland, in 1960, the statement emphasized that the search for unity needed to be undertaken both in local settings and at a global level. This part of the text, since then often repeated, said: "We believe that the unity which is both God's will and his gift to his Church is being made visible as all in each place who are baptized into Jesus Christ and

---

1. Quoted in James W. Kennedy, *No Darkness at All: An Account of the New Delhi Assembly of the World Council of Churches* (St. Louis: Bethany, 1962), p. 25.

confess him as Lord and Saviour are brought by the Holy Spirit into one fully committed fellowship . . . and who at the same time are united with the whole Christian fellowship in all places."[2]

The reference to "in each place" and "in all places" became one of those cases where phrases in the midst of an ecumenical document captured the essence of an important idea and then took on an enduring life of their own. For those who still possess an ecumenical memory, the New Delhi Assembly is remembered for this crucial emphasis declaring that the search for church unity does not just occur through the drama of high-profile, global ecumenical gatherings, but also must take place, simultaneously, in cities and local areas where congregations live in proximity to one another.

Fifty years later, with the development of councils of churches throughout the world at national and local levels, we may be tempted to pay little heed to the New Delhi statement. But in light of the dramatic changes in the geographical presence of world Christianity, and in view of the effects of migration from the global South to the North on the religious landscape in local areas, the New Delhi statement comes alive with new prescience and meaning.

The Ecumenical Frontier in Cities

One of the realities is that in the United States, immigrants are concentrated in certain states, and within them in major metropolitan areas. For instance, three-quarters of all immigrants are in these six states: California, Texas, New York, Florida, New Jersey, and Illinois.[3] Further, major cites become magnets for immigrants. Thus, Los Angeles has 19 percent of all Asian immigrants, and California has 39 percent of that total group. Los Angeles and New York are home to a full one-third of all foreign-born residents in the United States.[4]

Immigrants find their new homes both within major cities and in

---

2. Alan A. Brash, *Delhi 1961: A Report on the Third Assembly of the World Council of Churches, November 19–December 6, 1961* (Christchurch, N.Z.: Presbyterian Bookroom, 1962), p. 37. Also available on WCC website at: http://www.oikoumene.org/en/resources/documents/assembly/new-delhi-1961/new-delhi-statement-on-unity.html.

3. Jehu Hanciles, *Beyond Christendom: Globalization, African Migration, and the Transformation of the West* (Maryknoll, N.Y.: Orbis, 2008), p. 244.

4. Hanciles, *Beyond Christendom*, p. 245.

suburbs. Chicago, for instance, has 590,000 immigrants in its city limits, but 984,000 foreign-born residents live in Chicago's suburbs.[5] Nearly all the major metropolitan areas of the United States are home to concentrated groups of foreign residents, and this is particularly true of cities on the eastern seaboard and the west coast, and in places like Miami and Houston.

However, the last decade has also witnessed the rapid growth of immigrants in several cities through the middle of the country. Charlotte, Raleigh, Nashville, and Indianapolis all had more than 100,000 foreign-born residents by 2010, and cities with some of the fastest growth rates of immigrants in the past decade include Baltimore (72 percent), Orlando (71 percent), Las Vegas (71 percent), and Atlanta (69 percent).[6] Recall that about two-thirds of these immigrants are Christians, and thus are establishing mono-ethnic congregations, joining multiracial churches, and finding ways to nurture and deepen their faith with the community of believers in these cities.

This trend is even more pronounced in Europe. While in this book's previous chapters on the effects of immigration, the focus has been limited purposely to the United States, these same dynamics are discovered in Europe. Jehu Hanciles summarizes this as follows: "In Europe also, the new immigrants include large numbers of Christians whose presence has contributed to an explosive growth in the numbers of churches. Largely confined to major metropolitan centres, these immigrant congregations display extraordinary spiritual vigour and dynamism, in startling contrast to most churches within the older denominations."[7]

To illustrate the effect, on any Sunday in London it is estimated that more nonwhite groups are attending church services — 58 percent — than traditional English white churchgoers.[8] Similar situations are

---

5. From the website of the Government of Illinois, "New Americans: Office of Policy and Advocacy," under "Immigrant Demographics" tab: http://www2.illinois.gov/gov/newamericans/Pages/Demographics.aspx.

6. Audrey Singer, "Immigrants in 2010 Metropolitan America: A Decade of Change" (speech given to National Immigrant Integration Conference, October 11, 2011), available on the website of the Brookings Institution: http://www.brookings.edu/research/speeches/2011/10/24-immigration-singer.

7. Jehu Hanciles, "Migration and Mission: The Religious Significance of the North-South Divide," in *Mission in the 21st Century: Exploring Five Marks of Global Mission,* ed. Andrew Walls and Cathy Ross (Maryknoll, N.Y.: Orbis, 2008), p. 128.

8. Hanciles, "Migration and Mission," p. 128.

found in Amsterdam, Brussels, and other major metropolitan areas. Hamburg, Germany, for instance, has sixty African congregations and an African Christian Council. The Protestant Church in the Netherlands supports an organization called Samen Kirk in Nederland, which links together sixty-seven migrant churches. In Spain, 30 percent of the membership of the Federation of Evangelical Religious Entities is from immigrant groups originating in Latin America and Africa.[9] These developments, and especially the immigration of African Christians to Europe, have been studied for longer, and in far more depth, than similar movements in the United States.[10]

One of the most dramatic results of the immigration of African Christians to Europe is the founding of what is the continent's largest church, the Church of the Embassy of the Blessed Kingdom of God for All Nations, in Kiev, Ukraine. Pastor Sunday Adelaja, a Pentecostal from Nigeria, started the church with 7 people in 1993. Today it claims 25,000 members in Kiev alone, and has started hundreds of "daughter churches." Ten years ago, its outreach strategy began focusing on marginalized groups and those suffering from poverty and addictions. Up to 90 percent of its membership is Ukrainian or Eastern European.[11]

When the WCC delegates in New Delhi approved the assembly's Statement on Unity in 1961, no one could have imagined how world Christianity would change in the next fifty years. At the time of the assembly, mission agencies from churches in the West were flourishing,

9. Frieder Ludwig and J. Kwabena Asamoah-Gyadu, eds., *African Christian Presence in the West: New Immigrant Congregations and Transnational Networks in North America and Europe* (Trenton, N.J.: Africa World Press, 2011), p. 7. This recent, outstanding volume of essays originated from a conference on this topic held at Luther Seminary in 2007.

10. See Gerrie ter Haar, *Halfway to Paradise: African Christians in Europe* (Fairwater, U.K.: Cardiff Academic, 1998). This excellent account has since been followed by other essays by Gerrie ter Haar and the volume by Ludwig and Asomoah-Gyadu, *African Christian Presence in the West.* Pages 8-10 in the introduction to their book include an impressive description of the various conferences and research efforts centering on the religious dimensions of immigration to Europe from Africa, and the book contains five case studies from Europe. In a similar way, Afeosemime U. Adogame, Roswith I. H. Gerloff, and Klaus Hock, eds., *Christianity in Africa and the African Diaspora: The Appropriation of a Scattered Heritage* (London: Continuum, 2008), includes seven essays covering examples of the Africa Christian diaspora in Europe.

11. Asamoah-Gyadu, "Mediating Spiritual Power," in *Religion Crossing Boundaries: Transnational Religious and Social Dynamics in Africa and the New African Diaspora,* ed. Afeosemime U. Adogame and James V. Spickard (Leiden: Brill, 2010), p. 97. See also Hanciles, "Migration and Mission," pp. 128-29.

with plentiful resources to send missionaries to countries in the global South and East. The eventual migration of Christians from those countries back to the West as "missionaries" within societies where Christendom has collapsed was never foreseen.

Yet, the words of the New Delhi statement have ecumenical wisdom transcending the historical contingencies of the time they were written. The efforts to search for and make visible the unity of the body of Christ must be rooted and take hold "in each place." As the late John Howard Yoder wrote in his last essay before his death: "If the dividedness of the body of Christ is to be healed, that must happen where it is experienced as a wound, and that is locally, where people who live together as neighbors and work together as colleagues are kept from worshipping together by constraints imposed from outside their shared world."[12] Explanations in the New Delhi statement make clear that "each place" can mean local situations, like cities, or even neighborhoods. This certainly includes efforts toward unity between congregations in cities and metropolitan areas.

Today's changed context, therefore, calls for establishing broadly inclusive ecumenical bodies in major metropolitan areas in the global North. This is one urgent example of what the call to unity *"in each place"* means for the church today. Cities like New York, Los Angeles, Houston, Chicago, London, Amsterdam, Brussels, Berlin, Paris, and many more hold within them an astonishingly vivid and almost fully representative presence of world Christianity. So in these places, and many others like them, the unity of the body of Christ must be discovered, nurtured, and celebrated.

These are new laboratories for a changing paradigm of ecumenism in the twenty-first century. Pathways and keys toward discovering the unity of the church at the global level could come from fresh and new initiatives within such urban centers. But presently this is far from an ecumenical priority. If a council of churches even exists as an effectively functioning body in such urban centers, immigrant congregations generally are not within its ecumenical purview.

Some instructive exceptions to this pattern exist in Europe. When the Council of Churches in Britain and Ireland was founded in 1990 (since reformulated as Churches Together in Britain and Ireland), it in-

---

12. John Howard Yoder, "On Christian Unity: The Way from Below," *Pro Ecclesia* 9, no. 2 (Spring 2000): 180.

cluded sixty-five African Independent congregations.[13] There are also a Council of Christian Communities of an African Approach in Europe, a Federation of African Christian Churches in Brussels, and a Conference of African Churches in Switzerland. One of the highest concentrations of Ghanaian Christians in Europe is in Hamburg, and the African Christian Council in that city describes its ecumenical task this way: "For us ecumene is not just theory but practice. We try to give ecumene a concrete shape in our everyday lives. Ecumene is communication, reconciliation, and liberation from the walls that have been erected by the scatteredness of Christianity."[14]

But on the whole, and especially in the United States, ecumenical imagination, already in short supply, doesn't extend to the enormously fruitful possibilities of creating new local places of ecumenical fellowship, mutuality, and mission among the rich diversity of congregations in major metropolitan areas. Yet, in the global North, this truly should be one of the frontiers and future pathways in the pilgrimage of Christian unity in coming decades.

Building a "Fully Committed Fellowship"

If this challenge is to be taken seriously, what would such a new ecumenical body actually do? How would it form itself? What would happen if, for instance, a commitment was made to start something like this in Houston; or in DuPage County, west of Chicago, now home to 171,000 immigrants; or in Baltimore?

1. Discover Who Is There

The first step is to discover the immigrant congregations that already are there, but unnoticed and neglected. This requires attentive work. Then, as in all ecumenical efforts, the beginning point is building relationships of trust. Any fund-raiser will tell you that "people give to peo-

---

13. Ludwig and Asamoah-Gyadu, *African Christian Presence in the West,* p. 7.
14. Deji Ayegboyin, "Colonization in Africa: The Local and Global Implications for Christianity in Contemporary Nigeria," in *Christianity in Africa and the African Diaspora,* p. 42.

ple," not to an organization that lacks a personal connection to them. The same is true in ecumenical work. People — including pastors and denominational leaders — join an ecumenical fellowship or council because they have developed trusted relationships with its key leaders. Relationships continue to define the foundation for any fresh effort to discover and make visible the unity of the church.

2. Listen to One Another's Stories of Faith

Next, beginning such a fresh initiative among those who have been unacquainted with one another, such as Orthodox priests, evangelical personalities, Korean pastors, Hispanic Pentecostals, African independent church leaders, Catholic bishops, Methodist ministers, African American pastors, Lutheran bishops, Indonesian Presbyterians, Nigerian Baptists, Coptic Orthodox Christians, and Kenyan Anglicans — which is just a sample of what would be readily found in a major metropolitan area — requires listening to one another's stories of Christian pilgrimage.

The practice of sharing those stories, discovered in the formation of the Global Christian Forum, is a simple yet powerful way to build trust that can transcend, or at least suspend, the multiple stereotypes, mistaken assumptions, and unspoken judgments that most will bring into the room. That practice should become a regular feature of such an ecumenical initiative.

Then, as trust begins to grow and the bonds of community begin to feel secure enough to be tested, such an emerging ecumenical body can enter into activities the participants can do together. The following are not in a sequential or prioritized order.

3. Enter into Theological Dialogue

One shared activity is deep theological exchange. The need for in-depth theological encounters between the churches today that define world Christianity, and are present in large urban areas, is essential. Later we'll explore this in some depth.

4. Work Together for Justice in the City

Possibilities of working together addressing specific areas of injustice, violence, and suffering within the city should be embraced. This might entail immigration issues, poverty, human trafficking, or local environmental destruction. The possibility of common ground for action in some of these areas is wider than some might assume. And when nearly all the churches in a city are united around a common social issue, they have a significant capacity to make a difference for the sake of God's kingdom.

5. Explore Common Mission and Evangelism

Such a growing ecumenical fellowship should explore areas of common witness, mission, and evangelism. Here is where the interchange can become especially engaging and creative. Many of the immigrant congregations in large cities convey the sense that they are part of a plan for carrying out God's mission in the United States, which they experience as a materialistic, hedonistic, secularized society. Some have been sent with that explicit purpose. Sharing that missional call with others, and discovering how churches well established in this culture respond, will be mutually enriching for all, and for the sake of God's mission.

6. Worship and Pray Together

Finally, all these actions must be undergirded by worship, prayer, and celebration. Once again, that presents deep challenges, but such a group will discover that some of its richest experiences come as participants learn how to pray and worship together. In Christian Churches Together in the USA, a national ecumenical body, we have adopted the practice of having each tradition represented by the five "families" — Catholic, evangelical/Pentecostal, historic Protestant, Orthodox, and the historic black churches — lead the worship in five separate sessions during the course of our annual meeting. That has proved more edifying than trying to put together a time of worship that seeks the lowest common denominator of elements that will offend no one.

And what is the goal and hope of those who are gathered together,

133

sharing life in one city, and praying for the sake of that city? First, that they might become "one fully committed fellowship." Here again we are drawn back to those words from New Delhi, describing what it means for those "in each place" to "be brought by the Holy Spirit into one fully committed fellowship":

> It is a fellowship of those who are called together by the Holy Spirit and in baptism confess Christ as Lord and Saviour. They are thus "fully committed" to him and to one another. Such a fellowship means for those who participate in it nothing less than a renewed mind and spirit, a full participation in common praise and prayer, the shared realities of penitence and forgiveness, mutuality in suffering and joy, listening together to the same Gospel, responding in faith, obedience and service, joining in the one mission of Christ in the world, a self-forgetting love for all for whom Christ died, and the reconciling grace which breaks down every wall of race, colour, caste, tribe, sex, class and nation.[15]

That is the vision at the heart of this calling that would seek to find expression in local metropolitan settings. This, then, would mobilize the churches in their mission and work together for the sake of God's justice in the city. The prophetic words of Jeremiah, given to the people of Israel when they became strangers and sojourners in a land not their own, would come to life: "Seek the welfare of the city where I have sent you into exile, and pray to the LORD on its behalf, for in its welfare you will find your welfare" (Jeremiah 29:7).

As one listens to the suggested dimensions of activity, namely, theological exchange, joint action, and common mission, undergirded by worship and prayer, an echo of the historic streams forming the WCC and shaping its life is clearly heard — Faith and Order, Life and Work, Mission and Evangelism, with common prayer and worship. This is right. The basic agenda of the WCC in these formative areas has not been its problem. It still holds as a coherent and compelling framework what we pray for the churches to do together, emerging out of their fellowship, or *koinonia*.

---

15. Report of the New Delhi Assembly, Statement on Unity. The quote is from paragraph 10 of the statement. Available on WCC website at: http://www.oikoumene.org/en/resources/documents/assembly/new-delhi-1961/new-delhi-statement-on-unity.html.

The pressing issue is, who are the partners participating in such an ecumenical agenda? That is the underlying challenge as the growing, emerging parts of world Christianity that will shape its future are generally not ecumenical partners in theological dialogue, or in shared actions for God's justice and reign in the world, or in common mission and evangelism. But revitalizing the vision of such unity "in each place" offers the hope of creating new, broadly inclusive experiences of such a fully committed fellowship. And as that happens, the ecumenical agenda, with its basic framework, will be enlivened, transformed, and radically renewed.

"Each Place" in the Global South

What has been outlined is a fresh ecumenical frontier "in each place" for those seeking to live out their witness in the cities of the global North, and particularly in the United States. But how does this challenge from the New Delhi Assembly relate to those in the global South? Clearly, that question can only be answered by the churches within those regions as they seek to discern what it means to form a "fully committed fellowship in each place."

Some observations, however, can be offered. In several national settings in the global South, important initiatives are being undertaken to build more inclusive expressions of ecumenical life. Often, the divides between mainline Protestant, evangelical, Pentecostal, Catholic, and Orthodox can be overcome in encouraging ways. In part, that's because some of these divisions have their roots in the global North and have been reinforced by the money and power of its churches.

Moreover, given the severe challenges to sustain the common good in their societies over issues like food security, health, and human rights, the divisions between evangelical, mainline, and Catholic and Orthodox become indefensible. Cooperative action frequently results.

In India, the National Council of Churches, the Catholic Conference of Bishops, and the Evangelical Fellowship of India have cooperated together in a "forum" addressing common issues, including situations where churches are being persecuted. Following the gathering of the Global Christian Forum in Indonesia, Christian groups there, which were previously divided into separate organizations along evangelical and ecumenical lines, united to create the Indonesia Christian Forum.

In several African countries, such as Kenya, Ghana, and South Africa, initiatives are being undertaken to broaden councils of churches or similar bodies to reflect a full participation of all Christian traditions. The global South already holds a majority of the world's Christians, and it will be interesting to see how growing numbers of churches there will create new ecumenical bodies at the local and national levels that will be free from divisions often imposed or reinforced by churches in the global North. Such developments could define how those churches discover what a "fully committed fellowship in each place" looks like in their various contexts.

The New Delhi statement also reminds us that we are "united with the whole Christian fellowship in all places." The revitalized search for unity in local places, where congregations interact with one another face-to-face, is accompanied by the search for unity at a global level. Both take place simultaneously in ways that mutually strengthen one another.

Thus, the work of the Global Christian Forum, described previously, becomes indispensable at the global level as it brings new partners, especially from the evangelical and Pentecostal communities, and particularly from the global South, together with Orthodox, historic Protestant, and Catholic representatives, with the hope of tasting a "fully committed fellowship." At the same time, the ongoing work of the World Council of Churches, carrying forth critical theological dialogue and working persistently for justice and peace, builds on its gains in the basic framework of the ecumenical movement, achieved from its past sixty-five years of commitment to the unity of the church. These complement one another in breadth and depth as the whole body of Christ seeks to be united "in all places."

CHAPTER TWELVE

The Spirit and the World
in the Twenty-first Century

The Theological Clash of Cultures

Now that Christianity is centered in the global South, and non-Western expressions of the faith accompany faithful Christian immigrants to the global North, a fresh theological encounter becomes possible, and is crucial. As Harvey Kwiyani explains, "Non-Western theologies are usually held in a subordinate position to Western theologies. . . . the new phenomenon of non-Western Christian migration to the West makes these questions more relevant. Non-Western theologies are no longer confined geographically to the Majority World. They abound in many Western cities. For Western theological discourses to ignore them is not just wrong. It is to fail to be relevant to the current Western context of cultural Christian diversity."[1]

What we are experiencing locally, if we are attentive to our newly arrived Christian neighbors, reflects how the realities of world Christianity are reformulating theological development. Andrew Walls puts it this way:

> The most striking feature of Christianity at the beginning of the third millennium is that it is predominantly a non-Western religion. . . . We have long been used to a Christian theology that was shaped by the interaction of Christian faith with Greek philosophy and Roman

1. Harvey Kwiyani, "Pneumatology, Mission and African Christians in Multicultural Congregations in North America: The Case of Three Congregations in Minneapolis and Saint Paul, Minnesota, USA" (Ph.D. diss., Luther Seminary, 2011).

law. . . . These forms have become so familiar and established that we have come to think of them as the normal and characteristic forms of Christianity. In the coming century we can expect an accelerated process of new development arising from Christian interaction with the ancient cultures of Africa and Asia, an interaction now in progress but with much further to go.[2]

The dimensions of this theological encounter are only beginning to be realized. Analyzing them in any full way is far beyond the scope of this book, yet this process of theological dialogue is under way, in both "conservative" and "liberal" settings.[3] But the heart of this theological encounter, in my view, lies in the clash in worldviews shaped by Western and non-Western cultures, which then influences the way in which the Bible is read, and faith is understood.

Consider, for example, how an African worldview shapes one's understanding. The noted African author John Mbiti, author of *African Religions and Philosophy,* explains that in the traditional African perspective, the distinction between the spiritual world and the material world, which we assume in the West, doesn't apply.[4] Harvey Kwiyani, who grew up in rural Malawi, describes this intersection of the spiritual and material in this way: "The religious world of the African is spiritually vibrant. As such, for the African, the spiritual realm is real — so real that life is not imaginable without it. Africans usually say that the spiritual realm is just as real as the physical one. It is only invisible, and even though the two of them are distinguished, they cannot be separated. They are inter-connected and they work together."[5]

2. Andrew F. Walls, "Eusebius Tries Again: The Task of Reconceiving and Revisioning the Study of Christian History," in *Enlarging the Story: Perspectives on Writing World Christian History,* ed. Wilbert R. Shenk (Maryknoll, N.Y.: Orbis, 2002), p. 1.

3. For an evangelical perspective, see as an example Timothy C. Tennent, *Theology in the Context of World Christianity: How the Global Church Is Influencing the Way We Think about and Discuss Theology* (Grand Rapids: Zondervan, 2007). In the ecumenical world, the Ecumenical Association of Third World Theologians (EATWOT) has functioned since 1976. "EATWOT members take the third world context seriously, doing theology from the vantage point of the poor seeking liberation, integrity of creation, gender co-responsibility, racial and ethnic equality and interfaith dialogue." Statement is from its website, "Who We Are": http://www.eatwot.org/index.php?option=com_content&task=view&id=12&Itemid=26.

4. John S. Mbiti, *African Religions and Philosophy* (New York: Praeger, 1969).

5. Kwiyani, "Pneumatology, Mission and African Christians," p. 24.

Such a worldview, embedded in various non-Western cultures, collides with worldviews entrenched in Western culture. Shaped by the Enlightenment and the modern era, what we commonly call a "secular" framework for shaping culture and society is taken for granted. Simply put, such a view seeks to understand and structure social, political, economic, and cultural life without reference to God, or any religious and spiritual realities. Religion is then confined to the private, personal sphere. Optional space for religious practice is certainly guaranteed, but it is also circumscribed, both intellectually and practically.

Thus, it's the division between the material and the spiritual that is emphasized, and the organizing principle for understanding reality becomes rooted in an empirical, materialist worldview. Science and technology develop from such a secular faith. In capitalist democracies, this meshes conveniently with a strong sense of individualism, where individual "rights" form the foundation of political governance, and the freedom of individual actors drives the market as the basis for shaping the economy.

Now, of course, a thousand qualifications are in order. One of the persistent tensions of both politics and economics is between individualism and community in shaping the common good. The frontiers of science raise issues of cosmology, and reveal unfathomable mysteries in the creation. Postmodernism is a rebellion against the closed system of Enlightenment categories.

Further, the liberating impulses of the Enlightenment and the development of modern political, economic, and social life overturned systems of hierarchy, oppression, and control that previously dominated societies in the West. Who would want to return to a society where religious reality was defined for all by the state, and where political loyalties, religious beliefs, and social practices were proscribed in ways that reinforced the power of rulers and were imposed wherever necessary by the power of the sword?

Nevertheless, the operating worldview that frames contemporary societies in the West is shaped by secular assumptions that reinforce a practical materialism and functional individualism. Spiritual realities, if affirmed, are consigned to a segregated, personal sphere. Inevitably, but in highly complex ways, this cultural worldview influences how Christian faith is understood and practiced. Individualism pulsates through evangelicalism's beliefs and practices. Modernism frames more liberal understandings of Scripture that try to demystify spiritual and miraculous accounts that cannot be comprehended by such a worldview.

In concrete terms, Dave Gibbons, pastor of New Song, an innovative, multiethnic church with sites in southern California as well as Bangkok, Mexico City, and London, says many around the world view expressions of Christianity in America as "a version of Christianity . . . with diminishing power and influence and filled with a lot of pride, self-centeredness, and wrongheaded metrics. Being part of the Western cultural machine, our American churches tend to gravitate toward the gods of pragmatism, materialism, and consumerism. And today, people around the world can't see anything supernatural about that. The global village is longing for something deeper."[6]

Again, volumes explore what is inadequately summarized in these few sentences. The point, however, is that non-Western Christianity brings a worldview and understanding of life that clash with the assumptions of modern life in the West, and collide with many theological viewpoints and practices of churches in the West.

Author and theologian Akintunde E. Akinade explains in this way the development of non-Western Christianity that, contrary to the predictions of Western observers, blossomed and flourished with the end of colonialism:

> Christianity has blossomed in societies outside the Western hemisphere and has become more powerful and nuanced in the process. The anti-structural character of the non-Western phase of world Christianity plays itself out in characteristics such as charismatic renewal, grassroots revival, massive exorcism, vibrant house churches, robust indigenization efforts, and effective lay leadership. Churches from the Third World are vigorously defining Christianity on their own terms. The new day that dawns will permanently alter the place and nature of Christianity in the twenty-first century.[7]

This is why fostering places and spaces that welcome the interaction between Christian traditions of the West, rooted in the established

6. Dave Gibbons, *The Monkey and the Fish: Liquid Leadership for a Third-Culture Church* (Grand Rapids: Zondervan, 2009), p. 22.

7. Akintunde E. Akinade, ed., *A New Day: Essays on World Christianity in Honor of Lamin Sanneh* (New York: Peter Lang, 2010), p. 5.

churches of the global North, and non-Western expressions of Christianity, emerging from the new geographical center in the global South, is so essential. That needs to occur in both local and global settings — "in each place and in every place." Andrew Walls expresses the hope that "Perhaps the largest issues for the Church of Christ in the twenty-first century will be ecumenical."[8] That must be the case if we are to participate in healing the divisions in world Christianity.

The Social Impact of Non-Western Christianity

Each summer I join a group of pastors and theologians in Yellowstone Park who share a commitment to the "missional church" movement. We also enjoy fly-fishing. Our mornings are spent reflecting on the Bible ("Dwelling in the Word" is the process we use) and discussing themes or ideas, often taken from a book one of us has been writing. Then in the afternoon we go to the Lamar Valley or other areas to fish for trout. Pat Keifert, one of the pioneers in missional church theology and practice, who teaches at Luther Seminary in St. Paul, Minnesota, initiated this time.

Brian McLaren, the noted author, often joins us, and one morning in the summer of 2012 Brian shared some of his experiences and writings. He told of being in Burundi, an African country afflicted by a terrible civil war between Hutu and Tutsi factions from 1993 to 2005, in which 300,000 people were killed. In 2005, Pierre Nkurunziza, who had led a rebel faction, was elected president by a wide majority, and he instituted a process of reconciliation with a cabinet of Hutus and Tutsis. He has led efforts in education, health care, and economic development in a process aimed at healing the wounds of the nation. Nkurunziza is also a "born-again" Christian, and his public faith has been a strong part of his leadership in a country that is 75 percent Christian.

McLaren shared about meeting with a group of younger pastors in Burundi. The evidence of spiritual revival and the growth of churches,

8. Quoted in Deji Ayegboyin, "Colonization in Africa: The Local and Global Implications of Christianity for Contemporary Nigeria," in *Christianity in Africa and the African Diaspora: The Appropriation of a Scattered Heritage,* ed. Afeosemime U. Adogame, Roswith I. H. Gerloff, and Klaus Hock (London: Continuum, 2008), p. 41.

as in much of Africa, were clear and to be celebrated. However, these young pastors were asking a more basic question. What was the actual impact of such religious movements on the social and economic well-being of the country? In other words, was this making a difference in the opportunities of people to live, and find concrete liberation from illness and poverty? Was a more just society being created? These young pastors were struggling to find answers.

That's the question most commonly raised by many observers when the picture of Christianity's dramatic shift to the global South, and the accompanying rapid growth of forms of Pentecostalism, becomes clear. What is the actual social, economic, and political impact of all this? Is this creating more justice in society? Or are we seeing heavenly minded forms of Christianity that have no earthly good? Even more severely, was Marx right after all about religion being the opiate of the people?

More to the point, what is the content of the gospel that is being preached? Isn't a lot of it the "prosperity gospel" that promises God will make you rich, in ways that require a contortionist hermeneutic of Scripture? And what about the influence of fundamentalist and often politically right-wing television preachers and evangelists from the North on the theology of growing churches in the global South? Doesn't their money and power still wield influence and control? Is this just another iteration of theological colonialism? These are serious questions requiring honest examination. At the same time, this line of questioning reveals a bias among some who have become habituated to their own stereotypes of evangelical or Pentecostal forms of Christianity, and now simply project those judgments onto the global scene. Important attention has been given to these questions not only by theologians and missiologists, but also by sociologists of religion in more recent years.

Donald E. Miller is professor of religion and sociology at the University of Southern California, and also director of its Center for Religion and Civic Culture. He's the author or editor of nine books, most of which examine various aspects of religious life, and he's a practicing Episcopalian. Tetsunao Yamamori is a noted Japanese scholar of social studies and author of numerous books. For seventeen years he served as president of Food for the Hungry, and presently he's a senior fellow at USC's Center for Religion and Civic Culture.

A few years ago, Miller and Yamamori embarked on a study drawing on 400 churches in the global South nominated as self-supported, growing congregations that were focused on serving the needs of marginalized, poor, and disadvantaged members of society. To their surprise, 85 percent of these congregations throughout Africa, Asia, and Latin America were Pentecostal. For four years they traveled throughout the world, conducting 300 interviews in twenty countries, to understand the dynamics, motivations, and effects of these congregations.

Their results became the basis of a revealing book, *Global Pentecostalism: The New Face of Christian Social Engagement.*[9] This is one of the most serious sociological studies of Pentecostal congregations around the world engaged in "holistic ministries" with those on the economic and social margins of societies. Its conclusions help answer questions about the impact of the growth of Pentecostalism in the global South on the welfare of those in its societies.

Miller and Yamamori call these congregations part of "progressive Pentecostalism," and they see this as the growing edge of Pentecostal development in the global South. These congregations are engaged in a variety of efforts, including education, health clinics, housing, food assistance, community development, microenterprise loans, job training, drug and alcohol rehabilitation, emergency relief, training in the arts, anticorruption efforts, election monitoring, and similar initiatives.[10] Such involvements usually arise out of solidarity with those on the margins, for often they are drawn into the life of such Pentecostal communities.

Other consequences are also noted. These communities provide a sense of self-worth and affirmation to those whose spirits have been crushed. As Marla Frederick, professor of African and African American studies at Harvard University, said in her review of *Global Pentecostalism:* "Life stories of participants illustrate what other social scientists have found[,] that the spiritual regeneration found in Pentecostalism inspires a sense of purpose and possibility in people who have been written off by society."[11] Rather than reinforcing a personal and spiritual detachment from the realities of society, a growing sense of indi-

9. Donald E. Miller and Tetsunao Yamamori, *Global Pentecostalism: The New Face of Christian Social Engagement* (Berkeley: University of California Press, 2007).

10. Miller and Yamamori, *Global Pentecostalism*, pp. 42-43.

11. Marla Frederick, review of *Global Pentecostalism*, by Donald E. Miller and Tetsunao Yamamori, *Journal of the American Academy of Religion* 76, no. 3 (September 2008): 996-99.

vidual empowerment and community support can lead to forms of civic engagement.

When exploring what lies at the root of a sense of social engagement within these Pentecostal communities, Miller and Yamamori point to the power of worship: "We believe that the root of Pentecostal social engagement is the experience of collective worship."[12] Their sense is that the power of personal transformation that is evidenced in the spiritually effusive style of worship provides the underlying motivation for the social engagement that is so apparent in the communities they studied.

Some clarifications are necessary in all this, however. Like others who have studied Pentecostal communities around the globe, Miller and Yamamori distinguish what they observe from the classic expressions of "liberation theology," particularly in Latin America. A phrase often repeated is that while liberation theology is about the poor, Pentecostalism has become the church of the poor. The systemic social and economic analysis undergirding liberation theology is typically not found in progressive Pentecostalism. The starting point is different. Pentecostal communities begin with the concrete experience of the poor in their individual lives, seeking to spiritually empower them through the life of a local worshiping community. If broader political engagement and social advocacy develop, and sometimes they do, they rise from the "ground up."

Further, as Miller and Yamamori describe the progressive Pentecostals that they discovered and studied, it's clear that these are only some Pentecostals. On the one hand, plenty examples of Pentecostalism can be found that continue to feature forms of eschatology and piety that totally remove followers from any meaningful social engagement. On the other hand, versions of the "prosperity gospel" abound, with a theology that seems almost like capitalistic gnosticism. These various forms of Pentecostalism are present in a myriad of ways.

Some observers argue that the Pentecostal communities that are more indigenous, springing up freshly from the soil of the global South, as opposed to those that are offshoots of traditional Pentecostalism in the North, are more likely to be deeply engaged with the lives of the poor and involved in movements of progressive social renewal. Harvey Cox, whose 1995 book *Fire from Heaven* was one of the early studies of global

12. Miller and Yamamori, *Global Pentecostalism*, p. 132.

Pentecostalism by a mainline or "liberal" theologian, more recently said this in his response to Miller and Yamamori's work: "Something very important is obviously going on in the Pentecostal movement. Although previously fixed on a strictly otherworldly salvation, now the example of Jesus' concern for the impoverished, the sick, and the socially outcast, along with the vision of the kingdom of God, has begun to play a more central role."[13]

As Pentecostalism continues to grow, and other forms of highly contextual, indigenously rooted, and spiritually expressive forms of faith expand through the global South, answers to the questions of how these forms of non-Western Christianity will impact the common good of their societies will become clear. Research in both the global South and the global North will go deeper, and accompany practice. Miller's center at the University of California, for instance, has launched a major, well-funded Pentecostal and Charismatic Research Initiative, and is supporting fascinating studies around the world. Its overall present assessment of the social and political impact of these movements should be instructive: "The sheer numbers of renewalists in the parts of the world where Christianity is growing most rapidly will inevitably influence the way economic development, religious authority and political power evolve in those regions. As members of these movements begin to shape civic institutions through their participation and activism, Pentecostal and Charismatic religion will likely become an important consideration in national and regional policy practices, particularly in the global South."[14]

But these are not simply developments to be observed in the global South. Once again, through the unexpected gifts of global immigration, these are realities to be encountered in the cities and communities of the global North. There's no doubt in my mind that we've been witnessing major movements in the United States to free the gospel from its domination by a nationalistic, materialistic, and militaristic culture. Further, the impulses that search for expressions of faith that bridge the unbiblical chasm between personal conversion and social justice grow stronger each day.

13. Harvey Cox, review of *Global Pentecostalism,* by Donald E. Miller and Tetsunao Yamamori, *International Bulletin of Missionary Research* 32, no. 2 (April 2008): 108.

14. From the website of the Center for Religion and Civic Culture, and its Pentecostal and Charismatic Research Initiative, under "Politics": http://crcc.usc.edu/initiatives/pcri/politics.html.

Beyond this, one can clearly see how a powerful, emerging movement of Pentecostal social engagement, changing lives and creating empowered communities of the Spirit, can be strengthened by the penetrating and revealing prophetic critiques of how ungodly systems perpetrate the suffering of those on the margins, thirsting for salvation. Likewise, the faithful, persistent witness of Christians to those in places of power, pleading the cause of the poor, could become so enlivened and transformed by the empowerment of the spiritually transformed voices of the poor.

So now, a genuine encounter between the emerging non-Western forms of faith and the various expressions of Christianity long resident in the United States can accelerate the work of God's Spirit, shaping faith for the twenty-first century that can engage the spiritual vacuum of the culture and drive the social and economic renewal of the common good. That is why it is so essential to create those fresh pathways and places that allow us to walk together.

The Wrong Place to Start

Theological and ethical engagement between the churches in the global North and non-Western churches in the global South is already under way, of course. But it has started, and gained public attention, at exactly the wrong place — over issues of human sexuality, and same-sex relationships in particular. The conflicts involved quickly garner the attention of the media, and that in turn begins to build a narrative and shape perceptions.

The outlines of the controversy are easily summarized, at least on one level. Most churches in the global South view same-sex relationships as unbiblical and immoral. For them the case is closed, and it's a straightforward matter of obeying the Bible. When they observe the growing social and political acceptance of same-sex relationships in Europe and the United States, they see it as another sign of a secular culture that has departed from moral underpinnings intended by God. Overall, the public acceptance of sexual promiscuity and a high divorce rate, accompanied by rampant sexual content in media and advertising, reflects the moral degeneration of Western culture. Condoning homosexual relationships is simply regarded as a further sign of this deterioration.

When such Christians from the global South encounter churches in the North that sanction same-sex relationships, even allowing the ordination of clergy who are openly gay, they are baffled. Their initial conclusion is that such churches have allowed the pressures of the secular culture to compromise their fidelity to Scripture on these matters. This may affect how they approach partnerships with various churches in North America and Europe.

It's important to note, however, that while those views from churches in the global South certainly predominate, they are not uniform. Contrary views from a few church leaders, such as Archbishop Desmond Tutu and others in South Africa, are widely known. In Asia, some minority theological voices have a more nuanced view. On June 22-24, 2012, "Amplify Life," an all-Asia open and affirming church conference, was held in Hong Kong, and respected theologians like Kwok Pui Lan have powerfully articulated supportive perspectives.[15] Yet, voices like these are departures from the clear norm in the global South.

The situation has become particularly difficult for those denominations in the United States with their own internal conflicts over sexuality that have deep connections or membership globally with churches in the global South. Most public has been the Episcopal Church, whose membership in the Anglican Communion has been under strain since its ordination of Rev. Gene Robinson, an openly gay priest, as a bishop. Some congregations have left the Episcopal Church as a result and attempted to place themselves under the authority of Anglican bishops from Africa who share their conservative stance on these issues.

Many denominations, congregations, colleges, and Christian institutions in the United States find themselves deeply divided over the issue of same-sex relationships, and the challenge of offering genuine hospitality to gay and lesbian individuals. The fault lines are well known. Adherence to what is seen as the clear meaning of biblical texts

---

15. Kwok Pui Lan now teaches at the Episcopal Divinity School in Cambridge, Massachusetts. In 2011 she served as president of the American Academy of Religion. Born in Hong Kong, she became a Christian and joined the Anglican Church as a teenager. She's the author or editor of fifteen books in English and Chinese. Her article in the *Witness* magazine is entitled "Gay Activism in Asian and Asian-American Churches": http://www.thewitness.org/agw/kwok051904.html. Her blogspot from July 19, 2012, "Free Community Church in Singapore," is a fascinating account of her speech to a Christian gay and lesbian community in Singapore: http://kwokpuilan.blogspot.com/.

is contrasted with pleas to place them in a historical context, like passages on slavery, and appeal to more general admonitions of love.[16] The acrimony, hurt, and divisiveness created by this ongoing debate are painfully on public display.

But why is this subject the wrong place to center the interchange between the churches of the global North and the fast-growing witness of churches in the global South?

First, the conflict over same-sex relations is the agenda of churches from the North. Simply put, it is predominantly the problem, or challenge, of these churches. For countless historical and cultural reasons, changing social attitudes and political accommodations regarding gay and lesbian persons, and the status of same-sex relationships, are being clarified in these Western, postmodern societies. The churches within those societies necessarily are deeply engaged in this process, and divided in their responses.

However, these questions are not high at all on the agenda of the churches in the global South. Their immediate concerns focus on endemic poverty, social marginalization, educational opportunities, and the need for evangelism, spiritual empowerment, healing, and the liberating power of Christian community. Their deep concerns for sexual purity often focus on marital fidelity, and in some cultures this presents perplexing challenges regarding traditional practices of polygamy.

When the stance over same-sex relationships becomes the crucible for forming interchange between churches in the global North and those in the South, we should be clear about whose agenda this really is. Whether conservative or liberal, or evangelical or ecumenical, before Christians from the North bring this question to the table, they should ask themselves how long their churches, habituated to assuming they are at the center of the Christian world, will continue to impose their vexing questions on the agenda of relationships with the new Christian majority.

Second, and more disconcerting, when the controversy over homosexuality is brought into the focus of North-South Christian relationships, factions in the North will attempt to use groups in the South to

16. From the wide range of books on the subject, see James V. Brownson, *Bible, Gender, Sexuality: Reframing the Church's Debate on Same-Sex Relationships* (Grand Rapids: Eerdmans, 2013). This new book distills the issues with keen discernment and invites both "sides" in the debate into a deeper biblical engagement that can enrich the dialogue in helpful ways.

further narrow ecclesiastical agendas. The pattern is becoming familiar. Conservative and evangelical groups who, faithful to their conscience, want to press denominational bodies to adopt their preferred stance on same-sex relationships will appeal to southern church partners to support their cause.

Politically, such a strategy may make sense. Certainly, it's easy to find agreement on biblical interpretation and moral application between these groups. Further, some church leaders from the global South are more than willing to cooperate and inject themselves into these debates. But deep relational damage can be done. The health of the global church, and the possibilities for creative South-North partnerships that serve the vision of God's kingdom, are severely diminished when those from the South become pawns in the ecclesiastical chess games of feuding factions in denominations and organizations in the North.

As Kevin Ward, who was ordained by the Anglican Church in Uganda, writes concerning the conflict in the Anglican Communion: "The present crisis can also be seen as part of an American culture war 'by proxy,' in which conservative Episcopalians, long disillusioned with the development of their church, have finally found in the Anglican church of Africa and elsewhere, allies for their struggle. What is certain is that the debate on homosexuality is not one which has arisen from within Africa itself."[17]

Third, beginning the North-South dialogue with sexual ethics runs the danger of creating stereotypes and blurring attention to the full range of social, theological, and spiritual contributions that the emerging churches in the global South can bring to the wider Christian community. Already one can see a pattern of some mainline or more "liberal" Christians from the global North, committed to the inclusion of gay and lesbian persons in all parts of the church's life, viewing churches of the global South through the lens of their traditional position on sexual ethics. A stereotypical image develops, equating these spiritually expressive new churches with older versions of American fundamentalism. They can be subtly dismissed as biblically naïve, theologically uninformed, and even "primitive."

What get missed, of course, are the new patterns of social engagement that are transforming communities from the ground up, and the

---

17. Kevin Ward, "The Empire Strikes Back — the Invention of African Anglicanism," in *Christianity in Africa and the African Diaspora,* p. 94.

growing models of holistic ministry integrating personal and social transformation. One only needs to look at the advocacy agenda of the World Evangelical Alliance, and the work of the Micah Challenge, to see the grounds for common witness that are possible between mainline Christians from the North and emerging Christian movements sweeping through many parts of the global South. But superficial judgments based on differences over same-sex relationships can obscure those promising prospects of unified work for social justice in other areas.

In the end, we are faced with clear and strong differences between a growing number of churches in the global North and the vast majority of churches in the global South over the question of same-sex relationships. Weighty matters of biblical interpretation, cultural developments, biological and social influences, theological understandings, and ethical frameworks are all involved. These issues are not likely to be resolved any time soon. They will persist. But they need not divide.

Placing these differences at the center of the North-South relationship is a deeply damaging mistake, for all the reasons mentioned. Nevertheless, that does not exclude us from engaging these differences with one another. When we create a full and truly mutual relationship, we will celebrate our commonalities and explore our differences, convinced that this is how the Spirit continues to lead us into truth.

The late John Howard Yoder expressed our obligation this way: "From the gospel perspective, disagreement calls us not to go our separate ways but to invest in reconciling dialogue at the point of difference.... That we can work together when we agree is not yet the gospel. That is sociological works-religion, something we can do for ourselves, in our own strength. The word of reconciliation, on the other hand, directs us to talk together when we disagree. The gospel is that despite ourselves, by grace, we have been made one with people with whom we were not one."[18]

Walking Together

The intersection between a post-Christian West and non-Western Christianity will be a defining ecumenical encounter of the twenty-first

18. John Howard Yoder, "On Christian Unity: The Way from Below," *Pro Ecclesia* 9, no. 2 (Spring 2000): 177.

century. How the churches respond to the new and formidable divisions in world Christianity, driven by the rapid shift of Christianity to the global South and then the East, will determine the authenticity and power of our global witness. Either we will discover a striking and powerful mutuality born from the work of the Spirit, uniting distinctive, incarnational expressions of the church as part of one body, or we will persist in an accelerating fragmentation of those hoping to be faithful, self-righteously imprisoning each other in theological, cultural, and spiritual isolation, with a witness so weak that it makes a public mockery of the promise of reconciling love.

Our time is not unlike another transition from Jerusalem to Antioch. It's hard to comprehend how Christianity in the West, with its proud history, its worldly might, its intellectual vigor, and its cultural treasury, is living its life in a well-protected bubble, preserved by its claim to universality, with impulses of empire and echoes of Christendom still subconsciously resonant, and sometimes blatant. But the rise of non-Western Christianity bursts this bubble.

The question is not whether either the heritage of Western Christendom or the emergence of non-Western Christianity is "right" or "wrong." The young Christians in Antioch never questioned whether the faith of the church in Jerusalem was true. Rather, the question was, and is, whether the Spirit continues to be at work whenever the gospel crosses cultural, social, and geographical boundaries, expanding the reach of God's love, and becoming incarnate again in his body.

That is when the miracle of mutuality can spring forth from God's grace. The new is not assimilated into the old. But neither does it remain separate. Rather, a new community, born of water and Spirit, and sustained by blood, wine, and Word, is created. The epistle to the Ephesians boldly calls this a "new humanity":

> For he is our peace; in his flesh he has made both groups into one and has broken down the dividing wall, that is, the hostility between us. He has abolished the law with its commandments and ordinances, that he might create in himself one new humanity in place of the two, thus making peace, and might reconcile both groups to God in one body through the cross, thus putting to death that hostility through it. So he came and proclaimed peace to you who were far off and peace to those who were near; for through him both of us have access in one Spirit to the Father. So then you are no longer strangers and

aliens, but you are citizens with the saints and also members of the household of God, built upon the foundation of the apostles and prophets, with Christ Jesus himself as the cornerstone. In him the whole structure is joined together and grows into a holy temple in the Lord; in whom you also are built together spiritually into a dwelling place for God. (Ephesians 2:14-22)

Andrew Walls, the interpretive pioneer of world Christianity, likes to refer to "Ephesian moments" in the pilgrimage of our faith. Our hope is that we may be at such a moment today, in the encounter of those Jerusalem-like churches of tradition and catholicity with the Antiochian churches of spiritual creativity and missional imagination. That encounter may occur at many places, locally and globally, as foreseen at New Delhi. But we know one local place will be in the major metropolitan areas now reflecting the global realities of world Christianity.

When Mark Gornik completed his amazing story of three African congregations in New York City in *Word Made Global* and reflected on what we could learn, he turned to what Andrew Walls had written earlier: "Like the old Jerusalem Christians, Western Christians (have) long grown used to the idea that they were the guardians of a 'standard' Christianity; also like them, they find themselves in the presence of new expressions of Christianity, and new Christian lifestyles that have developed or are developing under the guidance of the Holy Spirit to display Christ under the conditions of African, Indian, Chinese, Korean, and Latin American life."[19]

Our invitation in such a time as this is simply to walk together on a common pilgrimage. Like the two disciples walking together to Emmaus, we share with each other "all that is happening" in our attempts to follow Jesus. When we have accompanied one another faithfully and honestly, and come to a table to eat together, in grace-filled moments unexpected, we will suddenly know the very real presence of Christ in our communion with one another. Then we will race to tell others.

---

19. Andrew F. Walls, *The Cross-Cultural Process in Christian History: Studies in the Transmission and Appropriation of Christian Faith* (Maryknoll, N.Y.: Orbis, 2002), p. 78, quoted in Mark R. Gornik, *Word Made Global: Stories of African Christianity in New York City* (Grand Rapids: Eerdmans, 2011), p. 266.

The View from Ghana

The highway from Accra to Akropong stretches out toward the mountains, though the constantly expanding city accompanies its path. At the base of the mountain traffic stops as the driver of our van pays a young woman in a wooden booth the toll required, while police stand by, making the stop feel like a checkpoint. A huge billboard is suspended over the highway with a picture of Nana Akufo-Addo, the presidential candidate of the main opposition party in an election a week away. These words are featured prominently, next to the dynamic pose of the candidate: "'The Battle Is the Lord's' I Samuel 17:47."

Enterprise is everywhere. Small shops, many almost like shacks, sell goods and services, and many major intersections host a marketplace. Among the many shops and advertisements, some stand out, like the "Jesus Is Lord Business Centre and Internet Café." We pass the "Give Thanks to God Tailoring Shop," and the "Sow in Tears, Reap in Joy Welding and Pipe Fitting" establishment. One of the small stands offering bottled water, soft drinks, and fruit is "By His Grace Refreshments." A sign reads "Shower of Blessings Painter" with a phone number. Automotive needs can be met at "God Is King Motors — Car Dealers." Winding our way up the hill toward Akropong, we pass the "Riches of Glory Guest House" and the "Jesus Is Lord Fabric Shop."

The lines between the secular and sacred, and the material and spiritual, are drawn very differently here than in my culture. I posted a picture on Facebook of the "Princes Beauty Palace," just a modest wooden structure featuring these words above the door: "I'm Not Alone Jesus Is with Me." Immediately one friend responded, "Same in Sierra Leone," and another said, "Same in Uganda." In fact, it's the same

153

throughout much of sub-Saharan Africa, which is now 70 percent Christian. The signs of a non-Western worldview reveal themselves in simple but illuminating ways.

The Akrofi-Christaller Institute of Theology, Mission and Culture is in Akropong, up in the mountains; it is where twenty-two of us gathered from around the world for the Global Christian Forum's governing committee meeting. Andrew Walls, now eighty, also teaches here and spoke with us at the beginning of our work. With a historian's sweep of the last five centuries, he explained how migration from Europe to the rest of the world in all its forms, which created the world order as we know it, has come to an end. With it, that world order now is beginning to implode.

But now, vast numbers of people are moving from the South to the Western world, creating the experience of the world church in these places. Walls underscored how this is a unique development in modern history, comparing it to what happened in the early church at Antioch. A bicultural, biracial church was united in Jesus, who was both "Messiah" and "Lord." Even the new name they acquired at Antioch — "Christian" — is part Latin and part Greek. And the metaphor Paul used for the church changed from a "temple" to a "body."

I asked Professor Walls about the conflict in worldviews between Western and non-Western Christianity. Christian faith, he explained, is always incarnational; it must be embodied. There's no "generic humanity," only cultural-specific humanity. During the Enlightenment, Western Christianity faced a struggle, and established an Enlightenment type of Christianity. And the Enlightenment had a firm boundary between the empirical world and the spiritual world. Western Christianity even tried to police that boundary. But non-Western Christianity doesn't see that boundary in the same way. So Walls believes this is a time of theological renaissance in order to figure all this out, and we've got to do this as one body, together.

Some of those who will be part of this theological renaissance, I think, are the forty-seven African students who received postgraduate degrees from the Akrofi-Christaller Institute at its commencement ceremony, held while our committee was there. Masters of arts degrees were given in theology and mission, Pentecostal studies, Bible translation and interpretation, and African Christianity. Joel Carpenter, also on hand to deliver the commencement address, says this institute is probably the best center for "authentic African theology."

The graduation ceremony was held at Christ Presbyterian Church in Akropong, and the procession of faculty, graduates, and guests moved through the red-clay streets of the city, led by African drummers and the traditional dancing of women. Dr. Emmanuel Evans-Anfom, now ninety-three, and a noted educational leader in Ghana, received an honorary degree. In response he spoke of the "need to break the myth that Christianity was a European religion imported into Ghana."

This Presbyterian church in Akropong was a reminder of the continuing influence of mainstream denominations throughout Africa. Anglican, Methodist, Presbyterian, Lutheran, and other historic denominational traditions have tens of millions of members, alongside those who are part of African Instituted Churches.[1] Yet even in Akropong, with its strong Presbyterian heritage, the evenings during our stay were filled with exuberant sounds of revival services being conducted at a local Pentecostal church. Further, the mainstream congregations can't be compared to those in the United States; they bear the imprint of a distinctive expression of Christianity in Africa.

At the front of the sanctuary of this Presbyterian church, a sign hangs on the left-hand wall listing the "10 Achievable Goals" of the congregation in the next five years. These include:

> To equip every member to win souls for Christ and to disciple them effectively.
> To snatch as many as the devil has bound.
> To equip members to live victorious Christian lives.

That's not quite the language of the First Presbyterian Church of Pittsburgh. But then these following goals are included in the list:

> To empower children, youth, and women to fight for their rights.
> To care for the needy and the poor.
> To collaborate (with government and donor agencies) in the fight against poverty, ignorance and disease.

This combination of language with highly spiritualized terms sounding like "spiritual warfare" with clear injunctions to seek social

---

1. Philip Jenkins, "The African Mainstream," *Christian Century* 129, no. 22 (October 31, 2012): 45.

justice and empower the marginalized sounds dissonant, and even jar-
ring, to the ears of many in the West. But in countless African churches,
this often seems to flow together naturally.

The thriving churches in Ghana, however, face numerous divisions.
Five separate councils or associations are functioning, namely, the
Ghana Council of Churches, the Ghana Catholic Bishops Council, the
National Association of Christian Charismatic Churches, the Ghana
Pentecostal and Charismatic Churches, and the Council of Independent
Churches of Ghana. Some individuals, like Michael Tawai-Ransford, a
Pentecostal leader, are working hard to bring the leaders of these vari-
ous councils around one table, to be called the Ghana Christian Forum.
Rev. Dr. Kwaku Asamoa-Okyere, administrative bishop of the Methodist
Church, chairs its interim committee.

The vision catalyzed by the Global Christian Forum is finding expression in various national settings around the world. India was one of
the first, and an Indonesian Christian Forum was established following
the global meeting in Manado. As our committee met in Ghana, we received a similar report from Bangladesh, as well as hearing about exploratory conversations in Pakistan. Further, we finalized plans for a
2013 gathering in the Caribbean, bringing together the various voices
and groups in the Christian community throughout these islands; presently they function with typically entrenched divisions. In the United
States, Christian Churches Together was an early initiative demonstrating that Catholic, historic Protestant, evangelical/Pentecostal, Orthodox, and historic black churches could form a committed fellowship
and engage issues like poverty and racism. While still imperfect, it's an
instructive, inspiring model.

Thus, church leaders in Ghana and other African countries have a
variety of models to examine as they explore how to create initiatives
and structures in the African context that demonstrate the unity of the
body of Christ that is both a gift and an obligation. As sub-Saharan Africa now emerges as one of the strategic centers of world Christianity,
exploring these pathways will be a critical feature in the church's future
witness.

Since the Global Christian Forum committee was meeting in
Ghana, a dinner was arranged with as many leaders of the denominations and councils in the country as could be persuaded to attend. We
gathered at the Miklin Hotel in East Legon, a prosperous, upper-class
area of Accra. My table included Abbrey Kofi James, head pastor of the

Divine Builders Bible Church, and a graduate of the Akrofi-Christaller Institute. His iPad and smart phone kept him continually wired throughout the evening, and we quickly became Facebook friends. Such connectivity bypasses the limitations of landlines. *Time* magazine reports that by 2016, Africa will have 1 billion cell phones in use.[2]

Apostle S. T. Doku, president of the Council of Independent Churches of Ghana, also was at our table, and he stressed the harmonious and peaceful relationship between Christians and Muslims in Ghana. Other "apostles" were also at the dinner, along with bishops from churches of the mainline, Pentecostal, and African Instituted Churches. It's not at all clear how some of these titles are conferred, and how those carrying titles like "apostle" function. Church polity experts in the West would likely roll their eyes when faced with this scene. Yet, one can't help but hear echoes of the ecclesial language of the New Testament.

Some leaders were asked to share about the "state of the churches" in Ghana, recalling that in 1960, at the time of independence, Christians totaled 24 percent of the population. Today it's about 70 percent, the highest in West Africa. One was Jude Hama, for many years the director of Scripture Union in Ghana. The influence of such parachurch organizations in many African countries is enormous. Hama estimated, for instance, that 75 percent of the present leadership of the churches in Ghana were formed and nurtured in faith through Scripture Union or Inter-Varsity Christian Fellowship.

Listening to Jude Hama, I reflected on how genuinely delighted evangelical leaders of such organizations in the United States would be to hear his report. But later, those from Ghana were invited to ask questions of those of us representing the Global Christian Forum. Hama was one of the first. We're living globally with an unjust division of resources, Hama said. And the power and finances of Christian organizations remain centered in the North. Moreover, more economic resources, overall, flow out of Ghana than come into Ghana. Hama asserted that all this is still under the unjust financial structures first established at Bretton Woods and carried out today through organizations like the World Trade Organization. We need a more biblical and just system of international finance.

Jude Hama then asked what the Global Christian Forum could do

---

2. Alex Perry, "Africa Rising," *Time* 180, no. 23 (December 3, 2012): 34.

to address such injustice, including how this is reflected in the North-South divisions in the church. This illustrated the holistic nature of faith found so often in this continent. First, Jude Hama was speaking with the passion of an evangelical, stressing the crucial role of discipleship in the life of the church. Then he was speaking like an ecumenical advocate, prophetically attacking unjust global economic structures. And this seemed natural.

The Global Christian Forum has the capacity to at least bring the full spectrum of Christian voices around the table to address common issues. A major focus of the committee's time in Ghana was trying to identify the next steps in that process, which will include consulting with the WCC, the World Evangelical Alliance, the Vatican, and other cooperative partners. What's clear, however, is that a wide range of voices from the growing centers of world Christianity in the global South, whose countries are often those marginalized in the globalized economy, will continue to press the issues of justice as part of an integrated biblical witness.

The last day of our stay in Ghana, a few of us from the Global Christian Forum committee chose to visit the Word Miracle Church International in Accra. Its founder, Bishop Charles Agyin-Asare, had intended to come to the GCF world gathering in Manado, Indonesia, in 2011, but was unable to do so at the last minute. His church was first brought to the attention of the GCF by J. Kwabena Asamoah-Gyadu, now teaching at Trinity Theological College in Accra with a new chair for the Study of African Christianity.

The Word Miracle Church International is representative of a new group of megachurches in Africa and beyond. While charismatic in conviction and practice, it is not part of a traditional and large Pentecostal denomination, such as Ghana's Church of Pentecost, with 2 million members. These megachurches have developed more recently and maintain their independence, and often spawn many affiliated congregations.

The site of Word Miracle Church International was a former cattle and meat-processing center in Accra. We were met graciously by Bishop Ohene B. Aboagye because Bishop Agyin-Asare was in the Philippines conducting three days of teaching and healing services. The church's story is remarkable. Begun initially in Tamale, in northern Ghana, in 1994, it was moved by Bishop Agyin-Asare to Accra to center the ministry in the nation's capital. About 70 people formed the worshiping community.

Eighteen years later about 7,000 worship at the main center in Accra; Bishop Aboagye actually had to add up the numbers of those attending various services to answer my question. Two services each Sunday are in English and one is in Twi, a local language. Two more are in French, and a youth church and a teen church worship separately. The largest worshiping groups meet in the Perez Dome, still under construction; it's regarded as the largest auditorium in Ghana. The church's ministry extends through many "branches" — Bishop Abaogye estimates these to total more than 150 throughout Ghana — and in Accra alone those affiliated as "members" total 50,000.

We asked Bishop Aboagye what accounted for this remarkable growth and outreach. He responded, "Tangible miracles." The bishop explained that the Word is preached, and healings, with "signs and wonders," take place. Often a week is set aside for special services where miracles and healings are expected. The congregation also celebrates communion, baptism ("believers'," not infant), and anointing, and has a structure of boards as well as elders, deacons, and deaconesses.

Bishop Agyin-Asare has a worldwide ministry, having preached in fifty-two countries. Before going to the Philippines, he sent ahead DVDs of his preaching and teaching, and healing and miracles happened even before his arrival, according to Bishop Aboagye. Agyin-Asare has written twenty-five books, and you can follow him on Twitter, join his Facebook page, read his blog, and see the church's ministry on YouTube. His television broadcasts reach throughout Africa and also to the Netherlands and the United Kingdom. Most likely, he's one of the more interesting personalities in today's global church that you've never heard of.

The Word Miracle Church International is entirely self-sustaining, not relying on outside funding. We asked whether the majority of those worshiping were women, which is often the case. Bishop Aboagye said they had asked the same question, requesting men and then women to stand, and discovered that men were in the majority.

The church's "branches" have moved beyond Ghana into other African countries. They've also extended to Germany and Italy as its members include migrants on the move. Moreover, Bishop Aboagye told us about a member converted through the ministry of the church who led its youth ministry for several years. Then, more recently, he was sent as a missionary to Maryland.

While the story of Word Miracle Church International has remarkable features, it's not all that unusual. Megachurches like this are growing throughout the global South, with charismatic leaders, spiritually empowered ministry, and missionary outreach. Some fall prey to temptations of money, sex, or power, which can afflict any church, but others thrive and grow. These can become important centers of missional initiative in the emerging global church, but the challenge is to draw them beyond their highly independent structures into engagement and patterns of mutuality with wider expressions of world Christianity.

A Patient Pilgrimage

This brief and impressionistic snapshot from Ghana is simply a window to view some of the textures and emerging forms of Christian faith and practice in non-Western settings of the global South. Some from the established churches of the North, unconsciously shaped by Western culture, may want to rush to make judgments, and impose stereotypes. None of that is helpful. Rather, we need the patience required of any pilgrimage.

We are, beyond any doubt, at one of those hinge points in Christian history. When the Gutenberg Bible was printed, its eventual consequences were unimaginable. But the last five centuries have witnessed democratized expressions of Christian faith that have changed practices and spread experiences through the myriad languages and cultures of the modern world.

Now, an equally profound movement is occurring as the rising centers of Christian vitality have become detached geographically and culturally from the places in the North and the West that for so long have been Christianity's dominant, comfortable home. We can project the demographic features of this future. That alone is stunning. But it's far more difficult, and more decisive, to ascertain the spiritual, theological, and ecclesiological features of this future. Such discernment, however, is essential if the body of Christ, in the new, incarnationally inspired clothing of world Christianity, is to serve as God's intended vehicle for the world's healing, reconciliation, and salvation.

This discernment can only happen by traveling together on a common pilgrimage. The church's ecumenical calling, so central to its biblical identity and obedience, now becomes more urgent than ever, but also more urgently in need of refashioning its vision and practice to serve the whole church in the whole world.

Pilgrimages take time. They require a spiritual attentiveness to the landscape, and the shape of things encountered. An openness of heart and mind to unexpected discoveries along the way is a requirement. And perhaps most important, a disposition of solidarity and trust toward new companions, discovered as fellow pilgrims, often reveals the meaning of the journey itself.

So today's pilgrimage of world Christianity, from Times Square to Timbuktu and then back again, beckons us to join. The church, led by the Spirit, moves toward the future on pathways that often must be trusted more than they can be known. But we can be certain that these pathways can only be traversed together. In this time, when the seismic plates of world Christianity feel as though they are shifting beneath our feet, our call is to link hearts and hands across all that would divide us, and walk together toward God's future.

Bibliography

Adogame, Afeosemime U., and James V. Spickard, eds. *Religion Crossing Boundaries: Transnational Religious and Social Dynamics in Africa and the New African Diaspora*. Leiden: Brill, 2010.

Adogame, Afeosemime U., Roswith I. H. Gerloff, and Klaus Hock, eds. *Christianity in Africa and the African Diaspora: The Appropriation of a Scattered Heritage*. London: Continuum, 2008.

Akinade, Akintunde E., ed. *A New Day: Essays on World Christianity in Honor of Lamin Sanneh*. New York: Peter Lang, 2010.

Anderson, David A. *Multicultural Ministry: Finding Your Church's Unique Rhythm*. Grand Rapids: Zondervan, 2004.

Baptism, Eucharist, and Ministry, 1982-1990: Report on the Process and Responses. Faith and Order Paper, no. 149. Geneva: World Council of Churches, 1990.

Bilheimer, Robert S. *Breakthrough: The Emergence of the Ecumenical Tradition*. Grand Rapids: Eerdmans, 1989.

Brash, Alan A. *Delhi 1961: A Report on the Third Assembly of the World Council of Churches, November 19–December 6, 1961*. Christchurch, N.Z.: Presbyterian Bookroom, 1962.

Bunge, Gabriel. *The Rublev Trinity: The Icon of the Trinity by the Monk-Painter Andrei Rublev*. Crestwood, N.Y.: St. Vladimir's Seminary Press, 2007.

Cha, Peter, S. Steve Kang, and Helen Lee. *Growing Healthy Asian American Churches*. Downers Grove, Ill.: IVP, 2006.

Chaves, Mark. *American Religion: Contemporary Trends*. Princeton: Princeton University Press, 2011.

DeYmaz, Mark. *Building a Healthy Multi-ethnic Church: Mandate, Commitments, and Practices of a Diverse Congregation*. San Francisco: Jossey-Bass/John Wiley, 2007.

DeYmaz, Mark, and Harry Li. *Ethnic Blends: Mixing Diversity into Your Local Church*. Grand Rapids: Zondervan, 2010.

DeYoung, Curtiss Paul, Michael O. Emerson, George Yancey, and Karen Chai

Bibliography

Kim. *United by Faith: The Multiracial Congregation as an Answer to the Problem of Race.* Oxford: Oxford University Press, 2003.

Ebaugh, Helen Rose Fuchs, and Janet Saltzman Chafetz. *Religion and the New Immigrants: Continuities and Adaptations in Immigrant Congregations.* Walnut Creek, Calif.: AltaMira, 2000.

———, eds. *Religion across Borders: Transnational Immigrant Networks.* Walnut Creek, Calif.: AltaMira, 2002.

Eck, Diana L. *A New Religious America: How a "Christian Country" Has Now Become the World's Most Religiously Diverse Nation.* San Francisco: HarperSanFrancisco, 2001.

Edwards, Korie L. *The Elusive Dream: The Power of Race in Interracial Churches.* Oxford: Oxford University Press, 2008.

Emerson, Michael O., and Christian Smith. *Divided by Faith: Evangelical Religion and the Problem of Race in America.* Oxford: Oxford University Press, 2000.

Emerson, Michael O., with Rodney M. Woo. *People of the Dream: Multiracial Congregations in the United States.* Princeton: Princeton University Press, 2006.

Foley, Michael W., and Dean R. Hoge. *Religion and the New Immigrants: How Faith Communities Form Our Newest Citizens.* Oxford: Oxford University Press, 2007.

Gibbons, Dave. *The Monkey and the Fish: Liquid Leadership for a Third-Culture Church.* Grand Rapids: Zondervan, 2009.

Gornik, Mark R. *Word Made Global: Stories of African Christianity in New York City.* Grand Rapids: Eerdmans, 2011.

Griffin, Mark, and Theron Walker. *Living on the Borders: What the Church Can Learn from Ethnic Immigrant Cultures.* Grand Rapids: Brazos, 2004.

Groody, Daniel G., and Gioacchino Campese, eds. *A Promised Land, a Perilous Journey: Theological Perspectives on Migration.* Notre Dame, Ind.: University of Notre Dame Press, 2008.

Haar, Gerrie ter. *Halfway to Paradise: African Christians in Europe.* Fairwater, U.K.: Cardiff Academic, 1998.

Hanciles, Jehu. *Beyond Christendom: Globalization, African Migration, and the Transformation of the West.* Maryknoll, N.Y.: Orbis, 2008.

Heo, Chun-Hoi. *Multicultural Christology: A Korean Immigrant Perspective.* Bern: Peter Lang, 2005.

Howell, Richard, ed. *Global Christian Forum: Transforming Ecumenism.* New Delhi: Evangelical Fellowship of India, 2007.

Jacobsen, Douglas G. *The World's Christians: Who They Are, Where They Are, and How They Got There.* London: Wiley-Blackwell, 2011.

Jenkins, Philip. *The New Faces of Christianity: Believing the Bible in the Global South.* Oxford: Oxford University Press, 2006.

———. *The Next Christendom: The Coming of Global Christianity.* Oxford: Oxford University Press, 2002.

Johnson, Todd M., and Kenneth R. Ross, eds. *Atlas of Global Christianity, 1910-2010.* Edinburgh: Edinburgh University Press, 2009.

Kalu, Ogbu Uke. *The Collected Essays of Ogbu Uke Kalu: African Pentecostalism;*

Global Discourses, Migrations, Exchanges, and Connections. Edited by Wilhelmina Kalu, Nimi Wariboko, and Toyin Falola. Vol. 1. Trenton, N.J., and Asmara, Eritrea: Africa World, 2010.

Kalu, Ogbu, Peter Vethanayagamony, and Edmund Chia, eds. *Mission after Christendom: Emergent Themes in Contemporary Mission.* Louisville: Westminster John Knox, 2010.

Katongole, Emmanuel. *A Future for Africa: Critical Essays in Christian Social Imagination.* Scranton, Pa.: University of Scranton Press, 2005.

Keifert, Patrick R. *Welcoming the Stranger: A Public Theology of Worship and Evangelism.* Minneapolis: Fortress, 1992.

Kennedy, James W. *No Darkness at All: An Account of the New Delhi Assembly of the World Council of Churches.* St. Louis: Bethany, 1962.

Krabill, James R., ed. *Mission from the Margins: Selected Writings from the Life and Ministry of David A. Shank.* Elkhart, Ind.: Institute of Mennonite Studies, 2010.

Kujawa-Holbrook, Sheryl A. *A House of Prayer for All Peoples: Congregations Building Multiracial Community.* Bethesda, Md.: Alban Institute, 2002.

Lange, Ernst. *And Yet It Moves: Dream and Reality of the Ecumenical Movement.* Grand Rapids: Eerdmans, 1979.

Leonard, Karen Isaksen, Alex Stepick, Manuel A. Vasques, and Jennifer Holdaway, eds. *Immigrant Faiths: Transforming Religious Life in America.* Walnut Creek, Calif.: AltaMira, 2005.

Ludwig, Frieder, and J. Kwabena Asamoah-Gyadu, eds. *African Christian Presence in the West: New Immigrant Congregations and Transnational Networks in North America and Europe.* Trenton, N.J.: Africa World Press, 2011.

Miller, Donald E., and Tetsunao Yamamori. *Global Pentecostalism: The New Face of Christian Social Engagement.* Berkeley: University of California Press, 2007.

Min, Pyong Gap. *Preserving Ethnicity through Religion in America: Korean Protestants and Indian Hindus across Generations.* New York: New York University Press, 2010.

Myers, Ched, and Matthew Colwell. *Our God Is Undocumented: Biblical Faith and Immigrant Justice.* Maryknoll, N.Y.: Orbis, 2012.

Nelson, Dana K. *Mission and Migration: Fifty-two African and Asian Congregations in Minnesota.* Minneapolis: Lutheran University Press, 2007.

Noll, Mark A. *The New Shape of World Christianity: How American Experience Reflects Global Faith.* Downers Grove, Ill.: IVP Academic, 2009.

Ogungbile, David O., and Akintunde E. Akinade, eds. *Creativity and Change in Nigerian Christianity.* Lagos: Malthouse, 2010.

Olupọna, Jacob Obafẹmi Kẹhinde, and Regina Gemignani, eds. *African Immigrant Religions in America.* New York: New York University Press, 2007.

Pobee, John S., and Gabriel Ositelu. *African Initiatives in Christianity: The Growth, Gifts, and Diversities of Indigenous African Churches; A Challenge to the Ecumenical Movement.* Geneva: WCC Publications, 1998.

Bibliography

Rah, Soong-Chan. *The Next Evangelicalism: Releasing the Church from Western Cultural Captivity.* Downers Grove, Ill.: InterVarsity, 2009.

Raiser, Konrad. *Ecumenism in Transition: A Paradigm Shift in the Ecumenical Movement?* Geneva: WCC Publications, 1991.

Rodriguez, Daniel A. *A Future for the Latino Church: Models for Multilingual, Multigenerational Hispanic Congregations.* Downers Grove, Ill.: IVP Academic, 2011.

Sanneh, Lamin O. *Disciples of All Nations: Pillars of World Christianity.* Oxford: Oxford University Press, 2008.

———. *Whose Religion Is Christianity? The Gospel beyond the West.* Grand Rapids: Eerdmans, 2003.

Sanneh, Lamin O., and Joel A. Carpenter, eds. *The Changing Face of Christianity: Africa, the West, and the World.* New York: Oxford University Press, 2005.

Shenk, Wilbert R., ed. *Enlarging the Story: Perspectives on Writing World Christian History.* Maryknoll, N.Y.: Orbis, 2002.

Soerens, Matthew, and Jenny Hwang. *Welcoming the Stranger: Justice, Compassion, and Truth in the Immigration Debate.* Downers Grove, Ill.: IVP, 2009.

Spellers, Stephanie. *Radical Welcome: Embracing God, the Other, and the Spirit of Transformation.* New York: Church Publishing, 2006.

Tennent, Timothy C. *Theology in the Context of World Christianity: How the Global Church Is Influencing the Way We Think about and Discuss Theology.* Grand Rapids: Zondervan, 2007.

Van Beek, Huibert, ed. *Revisioning Christian Unity: Journeying with Jesus Christ, the Reconciler, at the Global Christian Forum, Limuru, November 2007.* Oxford: Regnum International, 2009.

Visser 't Hooft, Willem. *Has the Ecumenical Movement a Future?* Atlanta: John Knox, 1974.

Walls, Andrew, and Cathy Ross, eds. *Mission in the 21st Century: Exploring Five Marks of Global Mission.* Maryknoll, N.Y.: Orbis, 2008.

Warner, R. Stephen, and Judith G. Wittner, eds. *Gatherings in Diaspora: Religious Communities and the New Immigration.* Philadelphia: Temple University Press, 1998.

What Kind of Unity? Faith and Order Paper, no. 69. Geneva: World Council of Churches, 1974.

Yoder, John Howard. *The Ecumenical Movement and the Faithful Church.* Scottdale, Pa.: Mennonite Publishing House, 1958.

Index

Aboagye, Bishop Ohene B., 158-59
ACT Alliance, 22
Adelaja, Pastor Sunday, 129
Africa, Christians in, 8; church growth, 17
African Christian Council, 129, 131
African immigrant Christians, 79-80; migration to U.S., 83-84, 86-87
African Inland Church, 63
African Instituted Churches (AIC), Organization of, 35, 85-87
"African Noel, An," 97
African Religions and Philosophy (Mbiti), 138
African spirituality, 138, 154
Agyin-Asare, Bishop Charles, 158, 159
Akinade, Akintunde E., 140-41
Akrofi-Christaller Institute of Theology, Mission and Culture, 154, 156
Akropong, Ghana, 153-54
Akufo-Addo, Nana, 153
American University, 91
"Amplify Life" conference, 147
Anderson, David, 113
Anglican Church in Uganda, 149
Anglican Communion, 16, 147
Antioch, 31-32
Apartheid, South Africa, 51

Apostles' Creed, 2
Argentina, 11
Armstrong, Dr. Anton, 96
Asamoah-Gyadu, J. Kwabena, 63, 121-22, 158
Asamoa-Okyere, Rev. Dr. Kwaku, 156
Asia, Christians in, 8-9
Asian Americans, 88-91
Atlas of Global Christianity, 1910-2010 (Johnson and Ross), 7-8, 12, 17
Azusa Street, Los Angeles, 107

Bam, Brigalia, 63
Bangladesh, 156
Baptism, dialogue on, 49, 76; ecclesiology and, 76
Baptism, Eucharist, and Ministry (BEM) (WCC), 48-49, 50
Baptist World Alliance, 16, 22
Barnabus, 32-33
Barna Group, 25
Barrett, David, 14
Barth, Markus, 36
Belhar Confession, 41-43, 47
Benedict XVI, 10-11; new cardinals and, 10-11
Bergoglio, Jorge, x. See also Francis I
"Betelehemu," 97
Beyond Christendom: Globalization,

African Migration, and the Transformation of the West (Hanciles), 83, 125

Bible, democratization of, 1-2; Giant Bible of Mainz, 1; Gutenberg Bible, 1-2, 4, 160

Billington, Dr. James, 91

Bitros, Rev. Daniel, 63

Body of Christ, unity and, 31, 33-34

Borozdinov, Vladimir, 115-16

Borrely, Father Andre, 101-2

Brazil, Catholic Church and, 10, 18

Bridgeway Community Church, 112-13

Brown, Raymond, 39

Budapest, Hungary, 7

Buddhism: in Asia, 9; in U.S., 81-82

Building a Healthy Multi-ethnic Church (DeYmaz), 111-12

Burrows, William, 45-46

Burundi, 141-42

Busan, Korea, WCC Tenth Assembly in, 21, 52, 53, 56, 76

Calvary Church, Kuala Lumpur, 21

Calvin College, 11; and Seminary, 102-3

Cambodia, 9, 117

Camino de Santiago, 44-45

Candler School of Theology, 83

Caribbean, 88, 94, 156

Carpenter, Joel, 11, 117, 154

Catholic Church, 9-11, 71; in Africa, 10-11; charismatic, 93; in Colombia, 10; ecumenism and, 23, 158; eucharistic sharing, 50; Federation of Asian Bishops' Conferences, 64; in France, 10; Franciscan Friars of the Atonement, 60; in Hong Kong, 10; India and, 10, 11; in Italy, 10; in Latin America, 9-10; in Lebanon, 11; in Nigeria, 10; in the Philippines, 11; Pilgrim Office, 71; Pontifical Council for Promoting Christian Unity, 23, 60, 67; racial diversity and, 108; in

United States, 10, 89, 93-94; U.S. Conference of Catholic Bishops, 100-101; Vatican II, 23, 126

Center for Religion and Civic Culture, USC, 142

Center for the Study of Global Christianity, 14

Center IIMO, Utrecht University, 65

Challiot, Christine, 98, 101-2

Charismatic, 60, 119, 158; Catholic, 93; numbers of, 17-18, 158; worship, 108. *See also* Pentecostal

Chaves, Mark, 108-9

Chile, Pentecostal Church of, 54

China, 67, 90, 124; Christians in, 8, 9; independent churches, 18

Chinese Americans, 90

Christian Churches Together in the USA, 133, 156

Christian Conference of Asia, 64

Christianity: colonialism and, 5, 9, 85, 140-41; conceptual adaptation of, 14-15; dynamics of, 2-4; global institutions, 16; Muslims and, 3; post-Western awakening of, 5; return to South and East, 11-12; shift of center, 4-5, 7-12; spread of, 3; Western, 139-40, 151-52

Christian Reformed Church of North America, 103

Christiansen, F. Melius, 96

Christ Presbyterian Church, Akropong, 155

Church: Toward a Common Vision, The (WCC), 50, 76

Churches Together in Britain and Ireland, 130-31

Church of Christ in Nigeria, 63

Church of Jesus Christ of the Prophet Simon Kimbangu, 35

Church of Pentecost, Ghana, 158

Church of the Embassy of the Blessed Kingdom of God for All Nations, Kiev, 129

Church of the Lord (Aladura), 84-85, 86

Church of the Savior, Washington, D.C., 35
Church of the Servant, Grand Rapids, 102-4
Colonial missionary movement, 18
Colonial rule: Christianity and, 5, 9, 85, 140-41; Japanese, 89; Pentecostalism and, 17; theological, 142
Community of Saint'Egidio, 60
Conciliar ecumenism, 46-47
Conference of African Churches in Switzerland, 131
Constantinople, 4, 7
Coptic Orthodox, 118
Cosby, Gordon, 35
Cote d'Ivoire, 86
Council of Christian Communities of an African Approach in Europe, 131
Council of Churches in Britain and Ireland, 130-31
Council of Independent Churches of Ghana, 156, 157
Council of Jerusalem, 32, 33, 105
Cox, Harvey, 144-45
Crossing congregation, Boston, 112
Cuba, 83, 91

Denomination, separation and, 13-15
DeYmaz, Pastor Mark, 106-7, 111-12
Disciples of All Nations: Pillars of World Christianity (Sanneh), 11
Divide, global North-South, 15-16, 151-52, 154, 157-58; bridging, 80; same-sex relationships and, 146-50; spiritual, 20-21; youth and, 26
Divine Builders Bible Church, 157
Doku, Apostle S. T., 157
Dominican Republic, 82-83, 91
Dutch Reformed Church in Africa, 41
Dutch Reformed Mission Church, 41

Eastern Orthodox, 75
Ecclesiology, 40, 49-50, 74-76; local, 97, 115
Eck, Diana, 81
Ecumenical bodies: building new, 131-34; in global South, 135-36
Ecumenical Centre, Geneva, 16, 51, 79, 98
Ecumenical fellowship: evangelism and, 133, 135; in global South, 135-36; justice and, 22, 51, 56, 133-35; Pentecostal, 24, 40, 53, 75; worship and, 60, 73-74, 105, 133
Ecumenical movement, modern, 5, 18-19, 21-24
Ecumenical Patriarchate, 71
Ecumenism, conciliar, 46-47
Edinburgh World Missionary Conference (1910), 8, 17, 18, 22
Edwards, Korie L., 114-15
Egypt, 84
El Salvador, 82, 91
Elusive Dream, The (Edwards), 114-15
Emerson, Michael, 107-8, 109
English as a second language (ESL) programs, 102, 103
Enlightenment, the, 5, 139, 154
Episcopal Church, 93, 112, 142, 147, 149
Ethiopia, x, 84
Ethiopian Orthodox Church, 117, 118
Eucharistic sharing, Catholics and Protestants, 50
Evangelical Alliance in Africa, 66
Evangelical Fellowship of Africa, 63
Evangelical Fellowship of Asia, 64
Evangelical Fellowship of India, 64, 139
Evangelical Lutheran Church in America, 48, 118, 119
Evangelical Pentecostal Mission of Angola, 54
Evangelicals, 16-17, 40, 45, 142, 157-58; Asian Americans, 89-90; ecu-

menical movement and, 19, 56, 61-66, 100; Federation of Evangelical Religious Entities, 129; global institutions, 22-23; individualism and, 139-40; Latinos in U.S., 93-94; location of, 10, 53, 55; megachurches, 35; multiracial congregations and, 106-7, 113; Pentecostals and, 18, 24; same-sex relationships and, 149; social justice and, 135-36

Evangelism, 77, 148; ecumenical fellowship and, 133, 135; personal, 63

Evans-Anform, Dr. Emmanuel, 155

Facebook, 26, 153, 157, 159

Faith and Order Commission (WCC), 48, 50, 60, 69, 76, 126

Faith narratives, 26, 64-65, 66, 72-73, 132

Federation of African Christian Churches in Brussels, 131

Federation of Asian Bishops' Conferences (Catholic), 64

Federation of Evangelical Religious Entities, 129

Fire from Heaven (Cox), 144-45

Food for the Hungry, 142

Ford, President Gerald, 117

Francis I, x, 11

Franciscan Friars of the Atonement, 60

Frederick, Marla, 143-44

"Freedom Is Coming," 97

Fuller Theological Seminary, 61, 83, 90

Generational divide, isolation, 24-26. *See also* Young people

Geneva, Switzerland, 16

Ghana, ix, 153-54, 156

Ghana Catholic Bishops Council, 156

Ghana Christian Forum, 156

Ghana Council of Churches, 156

Ghana Pentecostal and Charismatic Churches, 156

Ghana Pentecostal Council, 63

Giant Bible of Mainz, 1

Gibbons, Dave, 140

Global Christian Forum, 3, 24, 136, 156-58; in Africa, 62-63; in Asia, 64; Continuation Committee, 62; in Europe, 64; faith narratives and, 26, 64-65, 66, 72-73; founding, 60-62; global meetings, 65-67; in Latin America, 64; "Our Journey with Christ in Africa," 63

Globalization, 104-5, 122-24; Christianity and, 124; economic, 124

Global North church: building ecumenical bodies in, 130-31; character of, 19-20, 139-40; decline of, 12, 20; secularization and, 20, 139-40

Global Pentecostalism: The New Face of Christian Social Engagement (Miller and Yamamori), 143

Global South church: ecumenical fellowships in, 135-36; orthodoxy issues, 20; sectarian character, 20

Gordon-Conwell Theological Seminary, 14

Gornik, Mark R., 86-87, 118, 152

Graymoor Ecumenical and Interreligious Institute, 60

Great Hymns of the Faith (St. Olaf Choir), 96

Greenbelt Music Festival, 74

Guatemala, 83, 92

Guneratnum, Dr. Prince, 21

Gutenberg Bible, 1-2, 4, 160

"Haleluya! Pelo Tsa Roma," 97

Hallelujah! We Sing Your Praises (St. Olaf Choir), 97

Hama, Jude, 157-58

Hanciles, Jehu, viii, 83-84, 95, 125, 128

Hart-Celler Act, 87

Harvard University, 81, 90, 143

Has the Ecumenical Movement a Future? (Visser 't Hooft), 68
Hawkey, Jill, 22
Heo, Chun-Hoi, 105
Hinduism, in U.S., 81-82
Hispanic Americans, 91-94; Catholic Church in U.S. and, 93; justice and, 93-94; National Hispanic Christian Leadership Conference, 93, 94; theology, 93-94
HIV/AIDS, 22, 63
"Holy Trinity, The" (Rublev), 97-99, 115-16
Homosexuality. *See* Same-sex relationships
Hope College, 39
Hospitality, to migrants/strangers, 98-100, 111, 118-20; Pentecostals and, 119-20
Howell, Richard, 64

Illegal immigration, issue of, 100-102
Immigrants: concentrations, 127-28; congregations and hospitality, 118-20; identity, 122-25; as missionaries, 83-84, 87, 95, 125, 130; religious lives, 120-21
Immigration, to Europe, 128-29
Immigration, to U.S., 87-88; Asians, 88-91; Buddhists, 81-82; Christians, 81-83; from Cuba, 83, 91; from the Dominican Republic, 82-83, 91; from Egypt, 84; from El Salvador, 82, 91; from Ethiopia, 84; from Ghana, 84; from Guatemala, 83, 92; Hindus, 81-82; Hispanics, 91-94; illegal, 100-102; from Kenya, 84; from Latin America, 91-94; from Mexico, 82, 91-92; Muslims, 82; from Nigeria, 84; from the Philippines, 82; from Puerto Rico, 91
Immigration and Naturalization Act, 87
Immigration reform, U.S., 100-102

Independent churches, 17-18; in Africa, 18; in Asia, 18; Catholic Church and, 18, 89; in China, 18
India, 165; Catholic Conference of Bishops, 135; Evangelical Fellowship of India, 64, 139; Hindu immigrants, 81; immigrants to U.S., 82; National Council of Churches, 135
Individualism, 139
Indonesia, 132; Christians in, 9; Indonesia Christian Forum, 135, 156
Institutional isolation, 21-22
Interchurch Center, ix
International students, to U.S., 90
Inter-Varsity Christian Fellowship, 90, 157
Islam, 3; in Asia, 9. *See also* Muslims
Istanbul, 3-4

Jacobsen, Douglas, 17, 45-46
James, Abbrey Kofi, 156-57
Japanese colonial rule, 89
Jenkins, Philip, viii, 11
John XXIII, 126
John Paul II, 71
Johnson, Elizabeth, 98
Johnson, President Lyndon, 87
Johnson, Todd M., 7, 12
Justice, 50, 100-101, 158; ecumenical fellowship and, 22, 51, 56, 133-35; Hispanic Christians and, 93-94; ministries, 77, 110; racial, 41, 109, 115; social, 55, 145, 150, 155-56

Keifert, Patrick, 99, 141
Kennedy, President John F., 84
Kennedy, Robert, 88
Kenya, 84
Kimbangu, Prophet Simon, 35
Kinnaman, David, 25
Kirchentag, Germany, 74
Klineberg, Stephen, 88
Koran, 3

Korean Americans, 89
Korean Presbyterian Church in America, 89
Kuala Lumpur, Malaysia, 21
Kwiyani, Harvey, 119-20, 137, 138

Latin America: Christians in, 9-10; immigration, 91-94; Pentecostalism in, 10
Latino: Catholics, 93; Protestants, 93
Lewis, Rev. Jacqui, 108
Liberation theology, 144
Library of Congress, 1
Life and Work movement (WCC), 50
Lilly Endowment, 108
Lima Liturgy, 48
Ludwig, Frieder, 118
Luther, Martin, 2
Lutheran World Federation, 16, 23, 67
Luther Seminary, 118, 119, 141

MacKay, Dr. John, 91
Madrid, Spain, 7
Mainz, Germany, 1
Mandela, Nelson, 51
Mapping the Oikoumene (Hawkey), 22
Marx, Karl, 142
Materialism, 124, 139-40
Mbiti, John, 138
McLaren, Brian, 141-42
McManus, Erwin, 107
Megachurches, 35, 107, 158
Mehmed II, sultan, 4
Mennonite World Conference, The, 22, 68
Methodist Church, 156; in Sierra Leone, 86; World Methodist Council, 16, 22
Metropolitan ecumenical bodies, global North, 130-31
Mexican Americans, 92
Mexico, 82, 91-92
Mganga, Boniface, 96
Micah Challenge, 22-23, 150

Micah Network, 22
Middle Collegiate Church, 108
Migrants. *See* Immigrants
Migration, 154; Christian, 83; economics and, 94; to North, 80-83; world population of, 83. *See also* Immigration
Millennium Development Goals, United Nations, 23
Miller, Donald E., 142-45
Minneapolis–St. Paul, 118
Miracles, 159
Mission, 31-32; ecumenicalism and, 133
Mission and Migration: Fifty-Two African and Asian Congregations in Minnesota (Nelson), 118
Missions: colonial, 18; early church, 3-4, 33; immigrants as, 83-84, 85, 95, 125; modern movement, 13; multiracial congregations and, 109-10; non-Western, 95, 159, 160; white control, 17
Modern ecumenical movement. *See* Ecumenical movement, modern
Modernism, 139-40
Mongolia, 9
Mosaic multiethnic church, 106-7
Mosaix Global Network, 107
Mott, John R., 70-71
Mount Tabborrar, 85
Multicultural Christology (Heo), 105
Multicultural churches, 104-5. *See also* Multiracial congregations
Multicultural Ministry: Finding Your Church's Unique Rhythm (Anderson), 113
Multiracial congregations, 106-10; building, 111-13; characteristics of, 113-15; evangelicals and, 107; leadership and, 110-11; mission and, 109-10; Pentecostals and, 107, 119; reconciliation and, 106; theology, 108; worship and, 108-9, 113
Music, 73-74, 97; Greenbelt Music

Festival, 74; Wild Goose Festival, 74
Muslims, 9, 82; Christians and, 3, 157

Nagel Institute for the Study of World Christianity, 11, 117
Nathan, Rich, 107
National Association of Christian Charismatic Churches, 156
National Congregations Study, 108-9
National Council of Churches, USA, 46, 100, 126
National Hispanic Christian Leadership Conference, 93, 94
National Latino Evangelical Coalition, 94
"Natufurahi Siku Ya Leo," 96
Nelson, Dana K., 118
Nepal, 9
New Delhi Assembly, 126-27; statement, 130, 134, 136
New orthodoxy, 11
New Religious America, A (Eck), 81
New Song church, 140
New York City, African churches in, 118-19
New York Theological Seminary, 45
Next Christendom: The Coming of Global Christianity, The (Jenkins), 11
Nidaros Cathedral, 74
Nigeria, 84
Nkurunziza, Pierre, 141
Non-Western Christianity, 151-52; awakening of, 5; social impact of, 141-46
Nouwen, Henri, 98

"Oba Se Je," 97
Obwaka, Emily, 66
O'Connor, Elizabeth, 35
Ogere-Remo, Nigeria, 85
O'Neill, Tip, 97
O'Neill, William, 100

Organization of African Instituted Churches, 18, 68, 155
Oriental Orthodox, 75
Orthodox churches, 18-19; Coptic Orthodox, 118; Eastern Orthodox, 75; ecclesiology conflict in, 75; ecumenical movement and, 23-24; Ecumenical Patriarchate, 71; Ethiopian Orthodox, 118; Oriental Orthodox, 75; Pentecostals and, 55, 74; unity and, 40; World Council of Churches and, 23-24, 49-50, 55, 126
Ositelu, Prophet Joshua, 85
Ositelu, Rufus, 84-85
"Our Journey with Christ in Africa," 63
Oxford Mission Study Centre Report, 65-66

Pakistan, 156
Park, Jerry, 88-89
Passover, Feast of, 29
Pentecost, Day of, 30-31
Pentecostal, 17-19; in Africa, 17, 85-86; in Asia, 17, 18; Azusa Street, Los Angeles, 107; baptism, 76; Catholics and, 60; colonialism and, 17-18; ecumenical fellowship and, 24, 40, 53, 75; Evangelical Pentecostal Mission of Angola, 54; experience, media and, 121-22; globalization and, 124; growth in global South, 10, 124, 129, 142-45; hospitality and, 119-20; in Latin America, 10; Latinos in U.S., 93-94; liberation theology and, 144; megachurches, 35, 158; movement, 17-18; multiracial congregations and, 107, 119; Orthodox churches and, 55, 74; progressive, 143-44; prosperity gospel and, 142, 144; social impact, 55-56, 142-45, 146; WCC and, 54-55, 61-67, 157; World Pentecostal Fellowship, 24; worship and, 144

Pentecostal and Charismatic Research Initiative, 145
Pentecostal Church of Chile, 54
Pentecostal World Conference, 21, 54
Pentecostal World Fellowship, 21, 67, 71
People of the Dream: Multiracial Congregations in the United States (Emerson), 107-8
Pew Forum, 14; Religion and Public Life, 17
Philippines, 82; Catholic Church in U.S. and, 89; Christians in, 9
Pilgrimage, 6; of Christianity, 5, 7-12; Jewish, 28-29; unity and, 74; worship and, 73, 76
Pilgrim's Guide to the Camino de Santiago, A, 44
Pluralism, 83; genuine, 124-25
Pluralism Project, 81
Pol Pot, 9
Pontifical Council for Promoting Christian Unity, 23, 60, 67
Postmodernism, 139
Presbyterian Church in Ghana, 86, 155
Presbyterian Church (USA), 48
Prill, Thorsten, 110
Princeton Theological Seminary, 91
Program to Combat Racism, 48, 51
Prosperity gospel, 142, 144
Psalms of Ascent, 28-29, 73
Puerto Rico, 91
Pui Lan, Kwok, 147

Racism, 40-41, 109, 111, 156; immigration and, 87; Program to Combat Racism, 48, 51
Radical Welcome: Embracing God, the Other, and the Spirit of Transformation (Spellers), 112
Rah, Soong-Chan, 105-6
Raiser, Dr. Konrad, 61
Reagan, Michael, 40
Reconciliation, 105-6

Redeemed Christian Church of God International Chapel, Brooklyn, 86
Reformation, Protestant, 2
Reformed Church in America, 41, 47, 48
Reformed Ecumenical Council, 46
Reformed tradition, 40; in South Africa, 40-41; U.S. Catholic Church and, 49; World Alliance of Reformed Churches, 46; World Communion of Reformed Churches, 16, 22, 68
Regional ecumenical organizations, 22
Religion and Public Life, Pew Forum, 17
Rio de Janeiro, 10
Robinson, Rev. Gene, 147
Roeda, Jack, 103
Ross, Kenneth R., 7
Rublev, Andrei, 97-99, 101-2, 115
Rutter, John, 97

Sacks, Rabbi Jonathan, 99
St. Nicholas Antiochian Orthodox Church, 117
St. Olaf College Choir, 96-97
St. Paul's Cathedral, Boston, 112
Salguero, Rev. Gabriel, 94
Samen Kirk in Nederland, 129
Same-sex relationships, 146-50
Sanneh, Lamin, 3, 4, 11
Santiago de Compostela, 44, 50, 71, 74
Scholz, Robert, 97
Scripture Union, Ghana, 157
Secularization, 12, 139-40
Seymour, William, 107
Shank, David, 86
Social justice, 55, 135-36, 150. *See also* Justice
Southern Baptist Convention, 100
South Korea: Christians in, 9; church youth and, 25; denomina-

tions in, 14; Japanese colonialism and, 89
Special Commission on Relations with the Orthodox (WCC), 55
Speller, Stephanie, 112
Spiritual journeys. *See* Faith narratives
Spiritual warfare, 155-56
Stanford University, 90
Starr, Bill, 91
Statement on Unity (WCC), 126-27

Taiwanese Americans, Christians, 90
Taizé community, 26, 74
Tawai-Ransford, Michael, 156
Television, preaching, 35, 142, 159
Theology, 137-40; African spirituality, 138, 154; exchanges, 132; Hispanic, 93-94; liberation, 144; multiracial congregations and, 108; renaissance, 154
Thomas Jefferson Building, Library of Congress, 1
Thuma Mina, 73
Timbuktu, x, 8
Time magazine, 126, 157
Tompkins, Oliver, 69
Toronto Statement (WCC), 49-50, 55
Tretiakov Gallery, 97
Trinitarian love, 98, 101-2, 116
Trinity, 38-39, 97-98, 115-16
Trinity Theological College, Accra, 158
Tunnicliffe, Geoff, 21
Tutu, Archbishop Desmond, 147
Tveit, Olav Fykse, 54

Uganda, Anglican Church in, 149
United by Faith: The Multiracial Congregation as an Answer to the Problem of Race (DeYoung, Emerson, Yancey, and Kim), 106, 113-14
United Church of Christ, 48
United in Christ, 60

United Nations, Millennium Development Goals, 23
Uniting Reformed Church of Southern Africa, 41
Unity, church, 16-17; body of Christ and, 31, 33-34; in Ephesians, 35-37; as journey, 45, 77, 152; mission and, 31-33, 77; music and, 73-74; Orthodox church and, 40; Passover and, 29; Paul and, 33-35; Pentecost and, 30-31; Reformed tradition and, 40-41; repentance and, 30; salvation and, 37; shared experience and, 74; of the Spirit, 37-38; Statement on Unity, 126-27; Trinity and, 38-39; young leaders and, 71
University of Southern California, 142
U.S. Conference of Catholic Bishops, 100-101

Van Beek, Hubert, 62
Vatican II, 23, 126
Vietnam: Buddhist immigrants, 81; Catholic Church in U.S. and, 89; Christian immigrants, 89, 117
Vineyard congregations, 107
Virgin of Guadalupe, 93
Visser 't Hooft, Willem, 68, 70-71

Walls, Andrew, viii, 11, 12, 152, 154; ecumenical issues, 141; on theological development, 137-38
Ward, Kevin, 149
Warner, Stephen, 120
Wattson, Father Paul, 60
Way of St. James. *See* Camino de Santiago
Week of Prayer for Christian Unity, 60
Welcoming the Stranger (Keifert), 99
West Asia, Christian center, 7
Western Christianity, 139-40, 151-52
Wild Goose Festival, 74
Wood, Rev. Ekow Badu, 63

Word Made Global: Stories of African Christianity in New York City (Gornik), 86, 118, 152

Word Miracle Church International in Accra, 158-60

World Alliance of Reformed Churches, 46

World Christian Encyclopedia (Barrett, Kurian, and Johnson), 14

World Communion of Reformed Churches, 16, 22, 68

World Council of Churches (WCC), 14, 16, 19, 21-22, 67; advocacy work, 56; *Baptism, Eucharist, and Ministry (BEM)*, 48-49, 50; *The Church: Toward a Common Vision*, 50, 76; Common Understanding and Vision, 52; contributions, 47-52; denominational outreach, 54; Faith and Order Commission, 48, 50, 60, 69, 76, 126; future of, 53-54, 56; Geneva location, 56; Global Christian Forum, 54, 60-67; Jubilee Year, 53-54; Life and Work movement, 50; Lima Liturgy, 48; music and, 73; New Delhi Assembly, 126-27; Orthodox churches and, 23-24, 49-50, 55, 126; Pentecostals and, 54-55, 61-67, 157; Program to Combat Racism, 51; Special Commission on Relations with the Orthodox, 55; Statement on Unity, 126-27; Toronto Statement, 49-50, 55; World Pentecostal Fellowship and, 24; young leaders and, 71

World Evangelical Alliance (WEA), 16, 21, 67, 158; infrastructure and, 23; social justice and, 55, 150; young leaders and, 71

World Methodist Council, 16, 22

World Pentecostal Fellowship, 24

World's Christians: Who They Are, Where They Are, and How They Got There, The (Jacobsen), 45-46

World Student Christian Association, 71

World Vision International, 16

World Youth Day, 71

Worship, 93-94, 99, 102-4, 134; ecumenical fellowship and, 60, 73-74, 105, 133; multiracial congregations and, 108-9, 113; pilgrimage and, 73, 76; social engagement and, 144

Yale Divinity School, 3

Yamamori, Tetsunao, 142-45

Yego, Bishop Silas, 63

Yellowstone Park, 58-59, 141

Yoder, John Howard, 37, 130, 150

Young people, 124; faith narratives, 72-73; generational divide, 24-26; leaders, 71, 141-42; Taizé community and, 74

YouTube, 159